The Footbook of Zombie Walking

How to be more than a survivor in an apocalypse

Phil Smith

Published in this first edition in 2015 by:
Triarchy Press
Axminster
EX13 5PF, England

+44 (0)1297 631456
info@triarchpress.net
www.triarchypress.net

A catalogue record for this book is available from the British Library.

Paperback ISBN: 978-1-909470-87-3
ePub ISBN: 978-1-909470-88-0

Contents

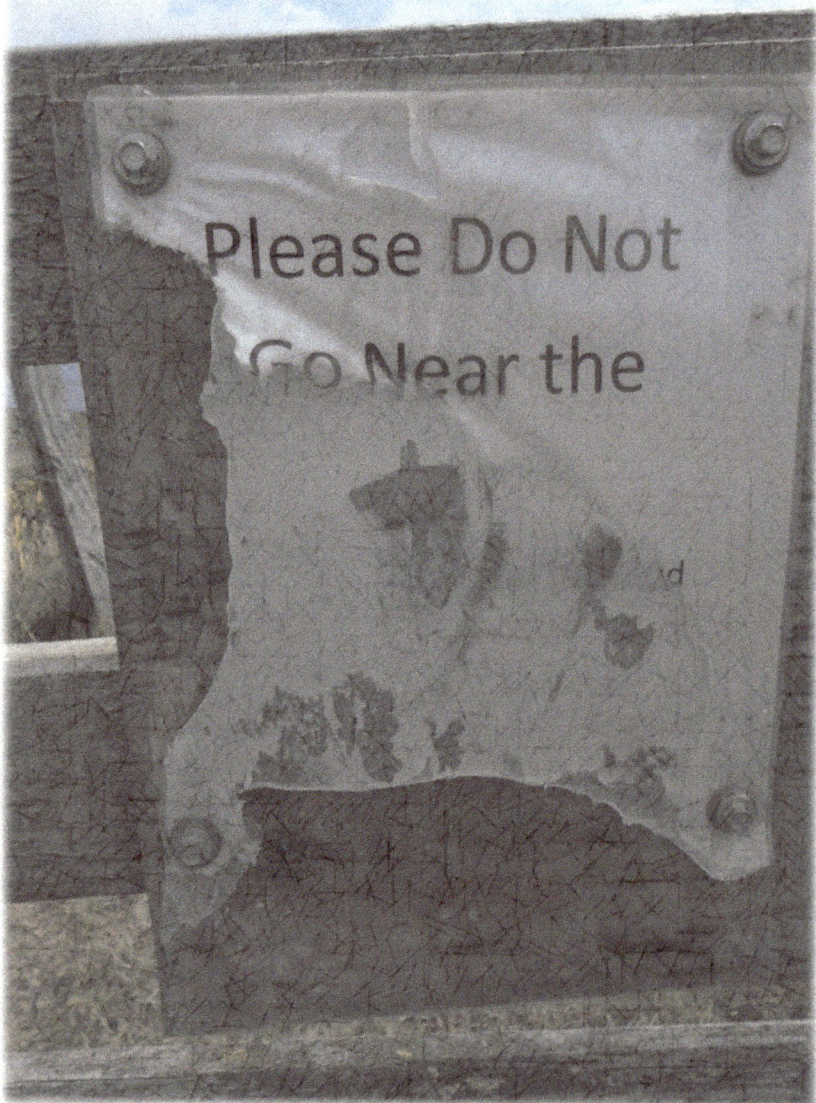

Introduction: acting in despair

I want to square a circle and make a common cause between devotees of the gentle arts of walking and fans of hyper-violent zombie fictions. It is a desperate act in desperate times: trying to weave together some serious thinking about the very particular era we have just entered with some exercises for the preservation of human consciousness in a world alight. All hung about a fictional apocalypse that is invigoratingly entertaining for many and intimidatingly morbid, or just plain tedious, for others.

Why try?

Because in zombie movies and comics, and not just the clever and innovative ones but in the offensively dumb and imitative ones just as much, by luck and art, there are hidden patterns of slowness, mindfulness and thingness, rigidity and softness, of fear, repetition and desire. These patterns offer maybe not hope, but a creative and ethical despair without which we will eat each other. And the only people who can stop us doing that are us. We are the people we've been craving for, the meat and potatoes that can do this, the dumbass zombie fans (like me) and the genius walker-artists (like me). Together, we can have a weird time on this planet-on-fire. We can learn how to walk with zombie secrets and go down with slow grace into the multiple mouths of disaster.

Walking plays a distinctive and controversial part in this myth. They are not the *walking* dead for nothing; disrupting the banality-inducing acceleration of images, the algorithms of the contemporary media spectacle and our headlong rush with our terrain to mutual annihilation. There is even a perverse crossover between zombie fandom and walking art in the form of zombie parades and flashmobs. So while I neither expect movie fans to turn into radical pilgrims nor ambulatory thinkers into gorehounds, at this moment in our global crisis… why not? Look around.

Illicit chemicals tear a district of a Chinese city apart in minutes. A *tsunami* (a word whose adoption into English we owe to an early researcher of colonial zombies) overwhelms a nuclear power plant; on a neighbouring continent blooms of jellyfish clog these plants' cooling systems.

Fundamentalist butchery dominates the waste lands of smoking infrastructure left 'shocked and awed' by US neo-con policies in the Middle East. The world 'achieves' its hottest year on record in 2014, and by mid-2015 a 'heat dome' has settled over the Middle East generating 'feel-like' temperatures in the mid-70s centigrade. In quiet English back gardens starving herring gulls tear puppies to pieces.

The arrest of black US citizens for minor violations repeatedly ends in their deaths. Yazidis, Copts and Chaldeans are systematically slaughtered, starved and sold into slavery. As Europe frays, the Ukraine splits and Greek banks close their doors to savers, at Calais and Kos human beings are forced to perform themselves as extras in disaster movies; on Turkish beaches sacred life becomes 'homo sacer' – the 'outlaw' who may be killed by anybody. The paucity of the slogan 'black lives matter' exposes how bare and impoverished human affairs are in some 'liberal democracies'. From the ruins of the Soviet empire a new cold war nuclear doctrine re-emerges. Chinese shares collapse. IS herds young women from minority communities in Europe to their territories to bring up the next generation for the Caliphate. Amazon sells rape guides. A former head of diversity for Google makes a planning application for a museum of women's history and opens it as a Jack the Ripper Museum.

Climate scientists, who have been telling us over and over that we cannot go on like this, have changed their tune: we have now gone on going on for too long, we have entered a new period of 'geological time' when human actions and the ecology of the planet are so entangled that what happens to us now happens to our world, and vice versa. That comforting 'get out of jail' card – if we just stop now the Earth can self-heal – is unplayable; our fanfare for this, and its self-important title 'Anthropocene', are parts of the hubris they denounce. James Lovelock's Gaia is out for revenge.

And you don't think this is the end for us? Perhaps you hope that it is your paranoia, rather than the ecology, that is out to get you?

Lists like the ones above have been and will continue, for a little while anyway, to be written; usually they are postscripted with 'but don't despair' and a counter list, often rather shorter and more general, of what 'you' can do; thinking globally and acting irrelevantly. Instead I am going to argue here: "and do despair". And that the other customary addendum (lifted from the Italian radical Antonio Gramsci) about "pessimism of the intellect, optimism of the will" can also be reversed. Think all you like but please stop trying to do things optimistically. Begin acting despairingly; that way our entangled world-selves might come out of this new 'end', this Sixth Mass Extinction, with a semblance of fecundity and even, if we are willing to go deep and dark enough, some fragments of sentience.

What I am proposing here is an agency of despair very different to the excited welcome that shock capitalism gives to disasters, ecological and economic; equally it is wholly unlike the old leftist revolutionary glee at each capitalist crisis as (finally!) the one to usher in an egalitarian utopia. Instead, action-in-despair takes place by slim chances and through very narrow windows of opportunity, has very little to do with ideals and more to do with 'making do', and will be mostly about repair and melancholy; something that has so far been more characteristic of paranoid far right survivalism rather than the excited and enlightened id of progress.

Inspired by a lack of ambition, optimism and prospects, I am proposing, perversely I hope, that the often dull and unprincipled patchwork presented here can still be enacted as a general 'art of living'; that repairs made stealthily in the everyday are the best we can, or should, do in an apocalypse which we are not always on the brink of, but that has been in motion for some time: "not... a crisis of capitalism, but rather the triumph of crisis capitalism... an endless end, a lasting apocalypse, an indefinite suspension" (p.25, The Invisible Committee).

The first step towards acting in despair is having the right apocalypse and there is no need to invent new ones. We have numerous varieties; none better and more immediate than the dominant fictional evocation of social chaos, extermination of human consciousness and the march to corporeal doom that is 'the rise of the living dead'. Among the virtues of adopting this particular catastrophe is that it shifts the ground of expertise away from the institutions of politics and academia to those lay experts – in the sense of laying on the sofa after the pub – immersed in popular film and genre fictions. Couch potatoes and walking artists can make a common cause in mimicking the universe, which is dying very, very slowly; cooling and decelerating by tiny increments, too full of mass to ever wholly freeze. An agency of despair draws on entropy rather than progress. And if any of this feels unrealistically pessimistic, just remember the chemicals, the butchery and the heat dome we started with. This is no longer about human survival. This is about how to go down best and most beautifully, most pleasurably and least hurtfully, while entangled in the reviving wreckage of the natural world as the moss retakes the sidewalks. It is not about heaven on earth, but about avoiding hell on earth in the interests of earth on earth. Acting in despair is to work asymmetrically; very carefully hitching a lift on the coat tails of disaster and slowing it down, not for better but for less bad. Inspired by the words of Samuel Beckett, who in this age of the 'Anthropocene' comes on like our beacon of active despair: "Ever tried. Ever failed. No matter. Try again. Fail again. Fail better."

The first figure appears in the distance

So, let's start again. But not from scratch.

The cosmos presents a map of itself to us. Through us. Every moment of every day, tiny and invisible ripples from the Big Bang pass through our bodies. Within these microwaves are temperature variations and, if we map these against the sky, they reveal a shape identical to the giant clusters of matter in the universe. These great structures of the cosmos, the meshworks that hold us temporarily in enough of a place to allow us a containable yet evolving life, are colossal fossils of energy spent long ago. And while the stars you can 'see' with the naked eye in the sky tonight are lights from suns that are still living (unless Eta Carinae has finally exploded), from far beyond them, and too dim for us to see unaided, come the last rumours of long dead giants. We make our various human ways – romantic, possessive, caring, creative, jealous, competitive, nurturing, violent – through an immense tomb, and all the time, it makes its way through us.

The modern zombie is a walking map of our world. As the universe presents its own representation of itself, so cinema is a moving representation of us, also from remains. Only the wavelengths are different. When the Russian revolutionary Leon Trotsky saw early silent movies in New York (he may even have acted in one or two) he remarked on how they made dead things of living beings, draining their colour and speech. More than 50 years later in 1968 (a revolutionary year), a non-character arrived to distil that revenant into itself: a reanimated, cannibalistic, monochrome corpse without a name (no one uses the word 'zombie' in 'Night of the Living Dead'). While this character emerges from a crowd of vampires, it also represents an unstitching of the monster of James Whale's 'Frankenstein', releasing its parts to swirl and crowd like the nebulous and confused 'people-monster', the Demogorgon of Percy Shelley's poem 'Prometheus Unbound', who when asked by Asia "who is the master of the slave?" can only mumble "If the abysm / Could vomit forth its secrets... / But a voice is wanting..." Since 1968, the modern zombie has relentlessly traipsed, "as inexorable as rain" (p.5, McHugh), deeper and deeper into more and more of our living and playing spaces, leaving rotting fragments of itself in the cracks in our cultures. How many people across the globe today are unable to define 'a zombie'?

Well, so much for all that. Any book on the living dead could have told you something like that. What comes now is different. There'll be no repeat of the zombie story over and over in ever more precise and comforting detail. Instead, a handbook for doing more-than-survive an apocalyptic culture; a set of tactics that adapts the walk of the zombie to the performance of the walking artist. I will draw inspiration and technique from the blossoming of these arts and performances over the last decade or so. I will take time out to describe in detail how certain zombie comics and films are inscribed with the secrets of our apocalypse, and how, if we unwind and rewind them, we can learn how to go less dangerously forward by slowing down our leaving of the past.

It would, of course, be good of me and convenient for you if I were to sum up in a few words what that "more-than-survive" might look like. But zombie walking doesn't work like that. You will be doing most of the walking yourself, out there on your own, or in a small band of squabbling survivors (just like in everyday life). You will be defining "more-than" for yourself, based on whatever that "than" refers to. For each reader it will be a different "more". And discovering that will be as much about walking as reading. Like a 'working' in alchemy, but with your body as the base metal, zombie walking is much more like living in a real catastrophe than moving your eyes across a page. At the same time, even for those of you who come at this from movie watching rather than extreme walking, I set out to redefine the meanings and significance of the living dead, bring its mythos closer to destruction, and show you things in the corner of the screen you will not have noticed before. By the finish – if you walk out of the other end of this book and there is no finish – the Night, Dawn and Day will all be a more entangled part of what you call yours. And the Land will call.

An awkward note

I have noticed that some writers on zombies (no names, no pack drill) like to reference a few movies or comics, launch a few metaphors (zombie as resilient other, as mindless body, as non-productive slave, and so on), and then ignore those narratives where the zombies have the gall to depart from their analysis. Others seem to regard the sub-genre as a cultural cake walk – "I love these movies because they reduce life to its simplest" (unpaginated, Jones) – or misrepresent – "without memory of prior life or attachments" (p.7, Luckhurst) – or idealise the zombie to fit their own politics – "by their lack of consciousness... [they] are immune to ideology" (p.9, Irven). This book is about the inconveniences. It is not about simple zombies. It is not about the zombie as slave and the living dead as exploited labourer and mindless consumer. Those are only our starting points, and I will struggle with just how complicated the bodies then get. Philosophising may be on the rough side here, devised on the run from monsters, offered up in fallen gobbets rather than triumphant formulations. I am not even sure if I end this book liking the living dead any more. Steering by their uncertain lights, including reflections on some of the 'classic' products as well as on a few lesser known examples, I will triangulate what I think of the living dead with my field notes from my own walking as a zombie in real towns and cities.

Fans and theorists alike tend to have their favourite version of the living dead. In my case I am favouring a surprisingly coherent Romero zombie (slow, democratic and with a dimly returning consciousness). If I did not know better I might propose this as the original, even 'pure', modern zombie, and later I will address exactly where such purity gets us. You will have to judge, then, if I am making sound arguments or exercising my prejudices.

I am assuming that you start here with at least some knowledge of the living dead. You don't need to be a specialist or expert in any way, not even an avid fan (though you can be, and it may help you to appreciate some of the detailed ideas here, though it might also hold you back in your comfortable expertise). The democratic nature of zombies is such that we are all, to some extent, expert in them. Whatever you may have seen or read, much or little, is canon enough for me. Where you might need a little extra information to 'get' a particular analysis, tactic or suggestion for adventure, I will give you what you require or directions for finding it. After that everything is up to you.

This book will not pretend to you that a zombie apocalypse is about to, or ever could, happen. In meat world things are much worse than that.

SPOILER ALERT!! SPOILERS THROUGHOUT!!

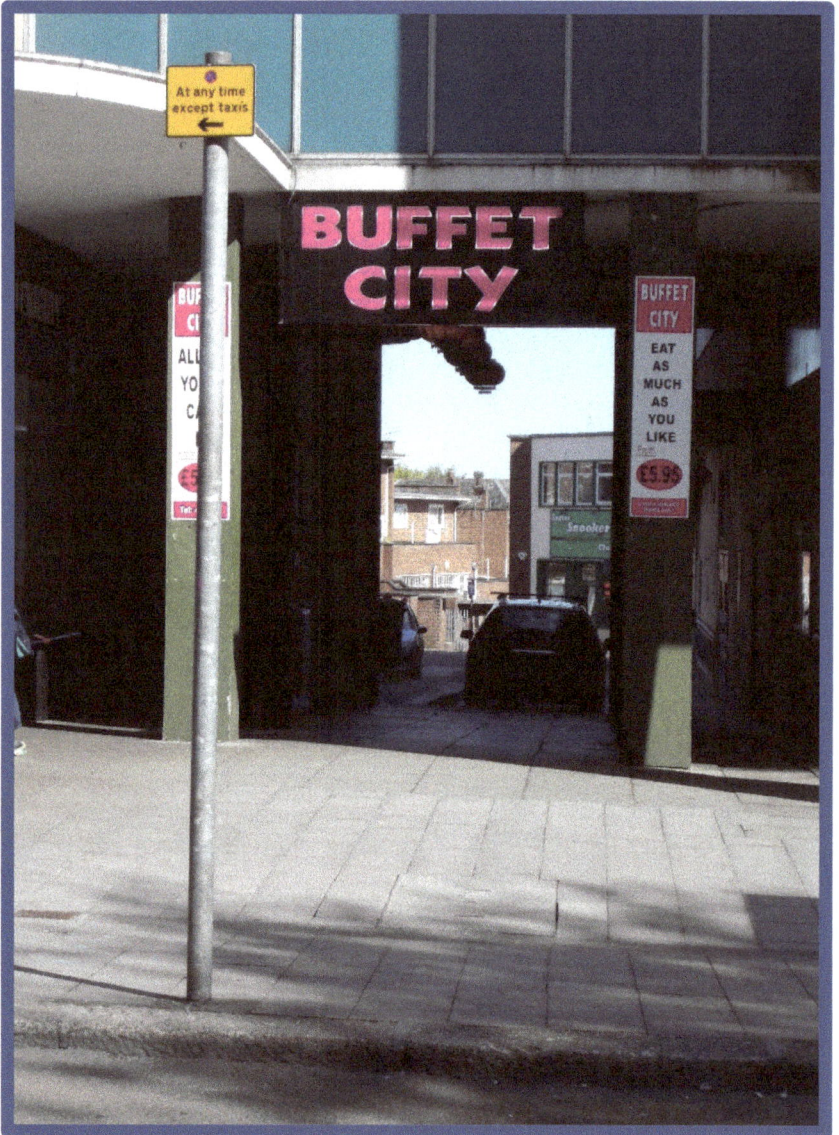

1/ the meat and potatoes

"A walk can be a dangerous thing" Judith Butler

In 2006 a collective of ambulatory artists called Wrights & Sites, of which I am a member, published *A Mis-Guide to Anywhere*. It is a guidebook for walking the world with alternative manners. As one of its many ambulatory tactics, the book suggests that we might all be 'Barbra'. The reference is to the lilting call "they're coming to get you, Barbra, they're coming for you", the aggressive-playful graveyard teasing of Barbra by her brother Johnny in the opening sequence of George Romero's now classic horror (but very much anti-classic at the time) 'Night of the Living Dead'.

The *Mis-Guide to Anywhere* suggests that the reader walk through familiar towns and cities *as if* they are Barbra; retaining their self-possession while looking through the eyes of a survivor in a catastrophe, not fleeing or attacking but observing like a movie camera from inside the head of a character, their senses heightened by the necessity to pay attention to the world.

> *Don't try to act or perform Barbra, or any character other than your own; instead, sensitise yourself to the atmospheres and derelictions of your everyday spaces; those grisly affordances and potent voids that you may have been editing out from your routine journeys. Walk carefully. Those around you may be predators, or survivors trying to put back together again the structures of life that got us into this mess in the first place. Avoid direct contact with others, whichever side of the living/living dead divide they might have fallen. Try to walk this border; sympathetic to both sides, respectful and wary of everything and everyone. Look for signs of an apocalypse that has arrived.*
>
> *And, most of all, listen to your feelings and the narrative <u>you</u> are writing in your head; as the 17th-century zombie hunter*

Defoe says: "WE'VE ALL GOT IT. BUT LISTENING TO YOUR FAMILY, YOUR PREACHER AND YOUR MASTER GETS IN THE WAY... LISTEN TO YOURSELF."

For the period of this simple exercise, don't follow your routine paths. Avoid linear routes and vary your trajectory repeatedly. Be aware of multiple escape routes, but don't necessarily take any of them. Escape is an over-rated affair; narrowing the field of vision in flight closes down the senses to points of departure. This will not help you in a world entirely infected; what you need is partial and conditional entanglement with everything. Porosity on your terms; not holes torn in you, but you opening yourself. To live in this slow apocalypse is all about finding a sustainable entanglement with as much as possible.

Jumps and scares will probably come along. Enjoy the rhythms of tension and relief. Rehearse shifting from a sudden jerk into a smooth continuation of your walk; taking these shocks into and in your stride. Be aware of what a space might suddenly produce; a large area of wasteground that could abruptly accommodate a crowd, corners that land you in the middle of a dozing horde, or an alleyway that could quickly become populated at both ends. Even water produces corpses; those cadaverous zombies that tip into New York harbour in Lucio Fulci's 'Zombie Flesh Eaters' are even now stumbling in the dark sludge towards a World Trade Center they will never reach.

Listen out for the natural soundtrack that the world is providing for you. The tense drone of ventilation units, 57 varieties of rustle in the leaves, the shriek of birds and the pylon hum.

Remember that the threat to you is fictional. And that fiction is a threat. Look out for all kinds of repetitious plots, seductive twists and cul-de-sac narratives. Navigate warily through hordes of commodities. Once you have made this walk, you have the basic building block of 'zombie walking'; everything else from now on will be either a variation on, or a repetition of, this 'meat and potatoes' walk.

In 1980 I came out of a cinema in the industrial city of Coventry in the English Midlands. I had just witnessed my first zombie movie: George Romero's 'Dawn of the Dead'. Prefaced by a low budgeted and laughable 'Giant Spider Invasion', I had been unprepared for the visceral shock of Romero's film. The mall scenes did not strike me as humorous; the bouncy rhythms of 'The Gonk' only served to heighten a sense of obliteration and abjection. When the blue-tinged corpse of an African-American project resident emerged from a flat to tear raw flesh from the shoulder of a family member, I felt that I had slipped into a wholly unfamiliar imaginary world. When I stepped outside into the sunshine at the end of the movie, uncomforted by the escape of two of the film's four central characters, what came as some relief was a recognition that the shoppers and office workers in the centre of my city did not move so very differently from the corpse hordes. I experienced an odd kind of return to normality. I was not horrified by the abjection of my contemporary and familiar city; I was excited and uplifted to be surviving in it. The horror I had seen in the darkness of the cinema was not from some other world that might at any time, in my head or through a screen or from some other gateway in the real world, emerge to invade this one, but had come from and had always been in this world; the underlying violence of its everyday. And that meant I could do something about it.

> Make your first zombie walk in territory you know well. Touch, sniff, watch these familiar spaces as if they were the setting for an apocalypse. Then try less familiar places. Walk as quietly as possible. Not on your toes. Put each heel down carefully. Choose each step and where you place it. Feel for the sonic qualities of what is underfoot. If you step on a snail shell today it will sound like a gunshot (yesterday, you wouldn't have noticed). Stop. Listen, get an idea of what the sonic background is; distant traffic, mystery rumbles, the absence of human voices. Sensitise yourself to any anomalies that cross this background. Stop again. Turn through the full 360 degrees, take in the horizon. Walk on very slightly tensed; ready to run, but not running.

> In one of the opening scenes of Romero's 'Day of the Dead' (1985) an alligator slithers from a doorway. Watch out for unexpected fauna and flora. 'Garden escapes' growing in the cracks on brutalist parapets, Himalayan Balsam squirting

their seeds beside culverts; deer, foxes, coyotes, snakes, scorpions and wolves in the city, peregrine falcons hunting from church spires, swarms of nesting herring gulls on tower blocks far from the sea and flocks of parakeets in the suburbs. Use cinematic eyes to seek out shifts in the pecking orders of these species and the overlappings of their territories; monitor their boundary disputes across the surfaces of boating lakes and ornamental fountains.

Ask yourself: why are zombies not walking birdtables smothered in feasting avians? Surely the birds would descend en masse upon such numbly unresisting and slow moving food sources? Carla Billinghurst's short story sequence 'The Usual Precautions' sends this up mercilessly in her portrayal of an Australian zombie outbreak; the local fauna make short work of the corpses. Picture passers-by as seething masses of beak and feather.

Once you are confidently tracking possible emergences of imaginary zombies from the architecture, then lay over those virtual trajectories the trails of tiny animals and the sky routes of sparrows and magpies. In the Argentinian-made 'What's Left of Us' (2013) we hear but never see the dogs that cry out in the city. It's the same for you: a sonic map rises to hover above the district you are in, the progress of unseen things recorded in barks and cries.

This kind of hyper-sensitised walking has something in common with what the disabilities activist and researcher Sue Porter calls "cripping the methodology"; equipping oneself with assumptions about the traps in the landscape that other viewpoints simply cannot see. Adopting the fictional apocalypse as a way of seeing, things that have been invisible or concealed will make themselves known.

One of the evolving sub-plots of the movie apocalypse is the gradual return of memory to the living dead. At the beginning of Romero's 'Land of the Dead' (2005), the giant zombie Big Daddy responds automatically to a gas station bell with a severed pump nozzle ready in his hand. In 'Day of the Dead', the decaying soldier Bub thumbs inquisitively through a Stephen King novel and attempts to shave. Fossils of living behaviour.

For some odd associative reason, I really don't know what, I get personally offended when critics and theoreticians write that the living dead have no memory. Partly it must be simple, empirical reasoning (see the paragraph above), but increasingly I realise that it is something more. It has something to do with comparisons. If the dead are so insensate and blank, how come their memories are elephantine in comparison with those Britons who now suggest that Syrian refugees should, like British citizens in the Second World War, stay in their cities (er, it wasn't a *civil* war in Britain in 1940 and no one *in* their cities wanted to kill them) or those citizens of the 'United States of Amnesia' (Gore Vidal) who could ask after 9/11 "why do they hate us?" when the list of US-invaded countries is longer than both their arms? The insult to the dead is all the greater when the comparison is made between their recovering memories (Bub's, Johnny's, all the rest) and those Coalition politicians (Blair, Bush, and all the rest) who lied and then couldn't remember the cover story. It is street wisdom – "if you're going to lie you better have a good memory" – yet such was their assessment of the people that they judged that they could skip that part of the assignment. What I am describing here is not a problem of zombie intelligence or unintelligent people – don't be tricked into thinking that this is a question of ignorance or stupidity; that way you will end up in sneering, prejudice and superiority under the guise of efficacy – no, this is something very sophisticated. This is about the making of ideology (which contrives to have no memory; in other words, it extends the lie to the lie itself, to what it believes, lying as it believes, and has no memory of its contriving), and it is ONLY the returning memory of one who has been abject, as if they had been dead to the world all these years, that can defeat that.

This is the potency of simple, meat and potatoes, being zombie.

Few who are exploited, economically or sexually or otherwise, do not know that they are. What sustains obedience and resignation is the reduction of that awareness to disconnected fragments, amputated parts of a commonsense that is no longer self-evident; dim recollections of resentments that have long been re-directed to something that is not their original cause. In the city, every day you will see bodies that snap at other bodies, stressed parents cursing their children, words left like teeth marks on the air; those that are loved and treasured (or simply and neutrally encountered) are made, just by their proximity, to stand in for those distantly hated and feared.

Check around you for re-enactments of 'what is done' and 'how things are', obedience to remnants of what is no longer believed in. Walk without trivial anxieties, selfish preoccupations and indifference, this is a city wholly alive with possibility and awareness. Who knows where the narrative will take you? Every bleak wall, every damp and stinking doorway, every wind-blown square is paused on the edge of mayhem and carnival. By running different scenes of apocalypse and zombie predation in your head, against the reality in front of you, you can explore this 'not yet' located somewhere between fiction and reality, near the border between living and dead.

You may find an odd satisfaction in the almost ascetic decency that the Romero myth introduced in 1968. A restraint within the excess that the philosopher Graham Harman calls 'sincerity': "not... that artworks need be prudish or morally upright, simply that they must be... truly wrapped up in being what [they are]... exhibit a genuine inner life of [their] own" (p.44). Such 'sincerity' is what the Romero zombies have – they "hold out the promise of being unleashed from the social and moral constraints that ambivalence bespeaks" (p.42, Rutherford). They are true to the little inner life they possess. The Romero zombie repeats and repeats its tiny and fragmented self, with discretion and consistency, in remakes and reboots;

Jennifer Rutherford characterises 'The Walking Dead' as "earnest". And what this sincerity wraps up and (en)grosses is us. A rotting arm reaching through the boards nailed over our inhibitions...

> *Despite the violence and bleakness of your starting point, there can be a surprising calmness within the zombie mythos, a falling away of ambitions and stresses, a peeling away of the future, a more intense being in the now.*

> *Zombie walking may lead you away from the busy hubs; to discover that, despite the tarmaced paths and well-worn tracks, walking routes are rarely busy places. Allow the imaginary threat to be your companion so that being alone is never a loneliness, but a dialogue with your imagination.*

> *Those of you who are already familiar with the 'drifts' I have described in 'Mythogeography' (2010) or tried the tasks in my book 'On Walking' (2014), can add 'zombie walking' as one more layer to your 'drifting'; for those who are trying this stuff for the first time, you have the advantage of novelty and unfamiliarity which each have their own impact. Whether a new or old hand, as much as possible, once you have the zombie narrative running in your head, let the spaces drive your walk and fuel your feelings.*

> *Whatever you lose in yourself by walking as Barbra, what you find outside yourself will more than compensate. Wandering in relation to the zombie, you do not have a destination. Avoid setting yourself targets; they become the claustrophobic cabins of your imagination. We know how that movie ends. Keep moving, stay nomad for the while you're playing this, repeatedly shift your relation to both built architecture and the natural world around you. Anticipate the rise and fall of the ground, read the shadows, learn how to look far ahead and up close at the same time, listen to the changing patterns of bird call and move in response to them, because they mean something.*

You are safe from horror, not, as the famous movie poster for 'Don't Look in the Basement' once advocated, by "repeating to yourself – it's only a movie... it's only a movie...'", but rather by admitting its reality and doing something about it.

2/ the body of the dead

"I want all the rich historical colouration to be manifest in talking about our finitude, being born of a woman in stank and stench, what I'd call funk, being introduced to the funk of life in the womb and the love push that gets you out, right, and then your body is not just death but the way Vico talks about it. Vico was so much better than Heidegger. Vico talks about it in terms of being a corpse, Heidegger doesn't talk about corpses, he talks about death, it's still too abstract – absolutely – read the poetry of John Donne, he'll tell you about corpses that de-com-pose, well, see, that's history, that's the raw funky stanky stuff of life, that's what bluesmen do..." Cornel West

As the eponymous hero of the movie 'Colin' (2008) begins to change, his movements assume something like the angular gestures of a body with disabilities. Or a dancer's exploration of possibilities. Once 'fully transformed' into living dead, Colin has the familiar lurch and stumble of the Romero zombie, but to get there he has fast-forwarded through an evolutionary history of variations and mutations hidden in his everyday body; as full of possibilities as an empty corridor lined with doors. This is the "nerve-wracking moment of transition... when a zombie is 'born'" (p.289, May), a moment too often now avoided in zombie-product. In increasingly action-based zombie films there is a tendency to pre-empt these transformations by swiftly despatching the bitten; these movies seem to baulk at the transgressive charge of a human self-revealing as the mother of its own self. Fear of the female, fear of motherhood, fear of the strange and the foreign, fear of the revelation of just how blank a space the self is, and fear of rampant and biological unhuman agency are all evoked in these scenes. But all this can be safely defused by turning the moment of 'birth' into the sudden opening of red eyes and biting jaws, human becoming animal, no more complicated than the nuts and bolts of Hollywood lycanthropy. How much more scary is that timidly enquiring mask of what was once Roger that slowly emerges from under his blanket in the original 'Dawn', unsure not only of where he is, but what he is.

Why are the shambling dead (almost) never pregnant? Is it because such a 'detail' would be extraneous? That they are all mothers of themselves?

When these zombie 'births' are missed out, pre-empted, speeded up as in '28 Days Later' or policed (by Andrea, for example, waiting by her dead sister Amy, gun in hand, in 'The Walking Dead'), then the mythos is harmed; like drinking coffee without caffeine, beer without alcohol, eating sweets without sugar or making revolution without doing violence to the self.

> *Take a walk to infect yourself with a new and alien idea, with a new and unfamiliar sensation, with a remote cultural ambience. Attend an event that is 'not you'. Enter a space to which you would 'never go'. Allow these differences to bite you a little. You don't need to put yourself in any danger, not even of changing your opinions; that is the potency of the zombie, just a little nip will do. Order a dish that you have never wanted to try. Once bitten, find somewhere to be quiet but not alone – a bench in a park or among the books in your local library – and let the you that had never done that thing, never reacted to that taste, never met those people, die a little. See what comes back from its grave.*

The make-up for the morgue-ready and emaciated zombies of Tom Savini's 1990 remake of 'Night of the Living Dead' were based on illustrations from pathologists' textbooks and footage from Nazi death camps. Dead ends. Like the wizened husks of Lucio Fulci's cemetery zombies. Savini's corpses are reaching for an uncanny that might lie closer to anatomical or taphonomic authenticity, yet, in trying for greater realism, they miss, with their elaborate scars and shrunken torsos, the everyday creepy ordinariness of the extras in Romero's original. The workaday clothing of the monsters in that originary movie (cast-offs donated by the extras themselves) – cheap business suits, pyjamas, vests, overalls, nightdresses, nakedness, slacks, surgical gowns – enhance the sense of ordinary bodies, clothed or unclothed, becoming extraordinary, fabrics no less vital than flesh: "dressing and being dressed... wrapping and being wrapped by fleshy tissues that have nothing organic any more, that cannot be distinguished from the clothing, the materials that usually hide them" (p.48, Perniola).

> *As you walk, feel your clothes fold to your body, stick to your skin, sense the tissues grip more tightly to your bones.*

Walking can transform the body: "folds of skin hanging from a skeleton. Eyes sunk in sockets like burnt holes in a blanket. Those delicate, sensitive artist's hands and fingers nothing but claws" (p.50, Haden); this is not a description of a zombie, but of the horror writer H. P. Lovecraft at the height of his walking mania.

> *The closing scenes of 'Resident Evil: Apocalypse' (2004) features some crawling dead who fasten hungrily upon a last villain standing. Strike a few blows against pedestrian-normativity. Against what Dee Heddon has characterised as the constant command of the healthy-walking lobby to "walk on!", a barely disguised "walk or else!" And against what Nick Land calls "spinal catastrophism"; the dominating and normatising upright walk. Re-take your walks at a crawl. Or as a crawl. What happens to your route when you have to worm yourself along on your belly, on all fours, or pull yourself along with Lovecraft claws? What happens to all those perpendicular buildings and upstanding citizens when you tip their world through 90 degrees? What happens to all your assumptions about what 'walking' is?*

What the movie 'Colin' nails but Savini and Fulci barely graze is a zombie-within. A zombie that is not a limping slave tied to the Past, but a figure of present crisis: a "crisis [that] is not economic, ecological, or political, [but] above all that of presence" (p.31, The Invisible Committee). This is not a spiritual crisis, but an existential one; it is a crisis of deep material bodies that have already escaped from the psychic force that Michel Foucault called "soul, the prison of the body" (p.30).

For, whether in the slopping viscera of 'Day' or in the enigmatic indifference of 'Night', what Romero gives his zombies is substance over both spectacle and mysticism, a communal and deep connectivity to all things, a thickness radically at odds with Andy Merrifield's strange call (given the antipathy to separation of his inspiration, Guy Debord) to "dethingify oneself... to create a separation... between form and content, between surface image and real underlying texture" (p.38). What the Romero zombie offers to the crises of existence, presence and interiority is a way back through deep matter, by the routes of things.

Thingify yourself.

No one ever skins a zombie; the abjection at its surface runs all the way through its body. It has no boundary or container; skinning is irrelevant to it. When Rick and Glenn cover themselves in viscera to pass for walking corpses, as if surface appearance and smell were what makes the zombie, the rain pours down its disapproval and washes off their disguises. There is no need for a "paradigmatic, almost generic" moment like that of Leatherface's skinning of LG and holding his facial skin up to the light in 'The Texas Chainsaw Massacre', "where the inside and the outside are revealed at one and the same time and when the permeable membrane between inside and outside becomes a metaphor for the movie screen itself" (p.151, Halberstam). In living dead movies, such a metaphor is just plain obvious; the screen oozes it, simultaneously explicit and opaque. What we see upon that screen is the thickness and thingness of an existential being that is skinned of its deceiving consciousness.

The living dead are crudely consistent, if they had minds sufficiently complex to choose (and we will see that some do) they would be highly principled; they are the same all the way through, subverting bio-illogically the old gothic trope of 'conflict in a single body'; hence, perhaps, their repeated coring, holing and cross-sectioning by humans. Their horror stems not from "identity and humanity become skin deep" (p.1, Halberstam) or from the ways that benign and familiar human appearances are shown to mask a vicious possession, but rather from the depth of flesh revealed throughout an ordinary body that is returning to life (as many, *qua* Freud, have pointed out, like a return of the repressed) and paroxysmed throughout with drive: "don't be excited by the old-fashioned idea that your body is reanimating and coming to life again, but by that more actual idea that you are sentient clothing" (p.48, Peniola).

> *But yours is not a zombie body. Zombie walking means animating your contradictions, your inconsistencies; it is walking with your viscera out, more sensitive and vulnerable than your surfaces, it is about leaving aside the mirror dance of everyday life and sinking its masks down through your body, dissolving the space between surface and innards, walking inside out. Walk aware of the weight of your different organs, not simply of the beat of your heart, but feel your heart pulling down on your ribs, your shinbone stabbing at the ground; savour the gravity of your feelings. Walk within your body; not a consciousness floating in a shell, but walk your flesh into the shape of a self, respond to the strain and decay already in there, the grind and the ache, the full meatiness and stringiness, all the parts beating and pumping together, in congress with itself. Practice spreading around whatever it is you find. Into your scalp, into your soles. Move the centre of your consciousness about; and then spread it to all the cells.*

I AM BACK
TO HAUNT
YOU!
NO MATTE
were you
HIDE
You You
will alway
Be lookin
OVER YO
Shoulde
Z

3/ is this it?

'El Desierto'/'What's Left Of Us' (2013) is a serious unpeeling of why survival is not enough.

Many are the writers who have pointed out that our horror at horror stories comes not from our fear of death, but from the fear that we talk far less about: that of becoming incapable of dying. Fear of a *wrong* survival. Shinji Mikami, the originator of the 'Resident Evil' computer game dubbed the sub-genre 'Survival Horror'. As Slavoj Žižek has it, "the obscene immortality of the 'living dead' which, after every annihilation, recompose themselves and clumsily go on... an uncanny urge to repeat painful past experiences that seems to outgrow the natural limitations of the organism affected by it and to insist even beyond the organism's death" (p.43, 2007).

The situationists, Parisian radicals who briefly made alliances with experimental artists from across Europe during the 1960s and inventors of the 'drift' (or 'dérive'), in their 'critique of everyday life' proposed that, with the advent of mass production and mass media, the entire 'developed' world had entered an era of just such 'wrong survival'. Despite the unprecedented surpluses generated by 20th-century production, no qualitative developments were happening; what was being produced was the quantitative accumulation of the means and behaviours of survival over and over and over again. 'Riches' were no more than pure surface; like the flaky "lamella" that Žižek describes above, they have no depth.

While Google can declare their intention to "solve death", media displays of shrinking ice fields and expanding deserts generate a grim satisfaction "derived from surveying the devastation of the environment... largely because it veils the shocking destruction of interiorities" (p.33, The Invisible Committee). The mirage of a technologically-enhanced 'immortality', of simply adding more and more years, is a feature of a spectacle of everyday life that is driven by accumulation; of gazes and images that are intimately linked to crude addition. Even while refugees from war and cultural genocides are risking their lives to find a way to Western cities, many of the people who already live there are troubled that, despite their relative wealth and comfort, their subjective lives are dominated not by eccentricity, creativity, indulgence or adventure, but with "the dull concern with survival, the economic worry about not having enough, the feeling of having an unsustainable form of life" (p.27). In flight and in war, bodies are threatened from without; in peace and rootedness they are hollowed from within: in both cases the same social relations apply, they are parts of the same system that reduces life to what is necessary – square feet, rent, oil prices, bandwidth, widescreen – and then multiplies or divides according to circumstances. Heaven now.

Lived on the surface, life, unsurprisingly perhaps, becomes a spectacle of itself; things and people (and the images of them) become separated, social relations severed; representation dominates the thing represented and the person who creates both thing and representation. It is this dominance of the surface of representations that constitutes the real threat in 'What's Left Of Us'; not the jaws of the dead. It is the appetite and longing for depth, however, that brings the film to its tragic (or as near as a zombie movie can be) conclusion.

In the movie, three characters – Ana, Jonathan and Axel – are holed up in a creaky but secure house, fortified against the undead roaming the streets outside; mostly unseen the zombies are occasionally heard. Sounds – gunshots, buzzing, feedback, barks, moans, breath – are important; the survivors have rigged up a microphone out on the street and monitor what it picks up. A reek of decay is evoked by the buzzing of flies and donning of half-masks.

The three living characters have acquired powerful weapons and developed rules of combat and a clear facility for responding to their predicament, but they are shorn of the bravado of vigilantes or the aggressive exoticism of 'zombie-hunters'. These survivors are as ordinary as the folks cooped up in the farmhouse in 'Night' though better organised and, fatally for them, more intimate emotionally. The ghoul that lurked in the cellar of the farmhouse, waiting for new recruits to its infection, was Family. It's there again at the beginning of the 'Dawn' re-make, and though she runs and drives furiously from it the other Ana in 'Dawn' cannot escape it in the mall, where it spawns a zombie child. In 'El Desierto' the desire for a secure and bounded social 'unit' dominates the lives of its survivors; to such an extent that when a human survivor speaks through the microphone – "Teresa – I'm alone... let me in... I've been walking for weeks" – Jonathan, at that moment on his own in the house, sends her away with gunfire for reply. In retrospect, given such indifference to other humans, we are led to suspect that the 'zombie', seen only from behind, killed by Ana in the opening scene of the movie, could also have been a living person.

Axel is having his body entirely tattooed with tiny blotches, as if he were breaking up into fragments or becoming human flypaper. He craves the sexual relationship that Ana and Jonathan have. Ana in her turn craves for the intensity of Axel but in the laid back Jonathan ("he fucks like an engineer"). Jonathan wants the continuation of all the bonding, urging Ana to take Axel as her partner should he, Jonathan, be killed – a suggestion as thoughtless as it is thoughtful. This could all make for yet another dull slough of soap opera clogging up a living dead movie, but by a subtraction 'What's Left' escapes all that: there are no TV channels accessible from the house.

There is nothing to tell the story of the outside world, only how it sounds and smells. There are no moving pictures. The spectacle of the city is mostly absent from the house. Instead, the characters become its spectacle for each other. As the movie's audience, we are equally denied a representation of the city: but for the briefest of street scenes at the beginning and a few snatched views of the skyline from the top storey, the camera never points away from the house. The intensity and significance of hearing emphasises the denial to looking. The gaze of the characters is concentrated inwards and increasingly upon each other and the contents of the house; the men play 'battleships' – a game in which the denial of a view drives the action – and Ana repeatedly thumbs through snaps of the old couple whose home they now occupy. All three make taped diaries, which Axel views (against the rules), and we get to see their relationships running at different speeds, in non-linear order, chopped up, de-composed. Ana catches Axel uncovering her body so he can watch her sleeping naked through plastic curtains; as if she were meat in a freezer.

Soon Axel and Ana are communicating mostly by taped message. Climactically, Ana herself becomes an invasive eye or camera, relentlessly and pointedly pursuing Axel through the house intrusively observing everything he does.

The challenge to survival in 'El Desierto' is less from risk to personal safety and more one of 'spectacle'. At one point the men, excitedly, get Ana to perform for them the private recording she has just made. Later, Axel will repeat back to her Ana's taped words to Jonathan as the couple made love in front of the running camera (against the rules). Ana only comprehends the intensity of Axel's feelings for her when she reviews his tapes; inside the house the performance and representation of intimacy circulates and predominates over intimacy itself. The 'spectacle', the domination of things by their images that has been enveloping the world economy since the entwining of mass production and mass media in the mid-20th century (now exponentially more powerful since global digitalisation), turns us ever more intensely towards a performance of ourselves. The image predominating over the flesh, the eye leaving, separating from and predominating over the body. (Read Jennifer Rutherford's chapter on 'Zombie Erotics' for a powerful description of how the spectacle can bear down on an individual playing at zombies.)

Ana is particularly sensitive to the malevolence of this gaze, both as a woman, and as a lonely child who feared the pitying gaze of others (the gaze of 'zombie humanism'); late on we see her, through the video camera, undo the strap of her bra, and then film only her eye in invasive close up. She performs the smile to the camera that Axel, to camera, had fantasised about her beaming directly on him. But even a friendly use of the recordings for communication is no less a burning away of desires than secret tapings.

The spectacle stands over our bodies and over the body of the city. In 'What's Left' the rooftop scenes are richly evocative of Michel de Certeau's critical account of a view of the city from above: "a way of keeping aloof, by the space planner urbanist, city planner or cartographer. The panorama-city is a... simulacrum, in short a picture, whose condition of possibility is an oblivion and a misunderstanding of practices. The voyeur-god created by this fiction... knows only cadavers" (pp.92-93). The walking dead rarely climb stairs unless in pursuit of a specific prey. They do not ascend iconic towers "to be lifted out of the city's grasp" (p.92), let alone to scan what is to be seen below. Rather, it is from the helicopter in 'Dawn', or the camera's bird's eye views in 'Nightmare City' and the 'Dawn' remake, that the viewer is given these vistas; a concussed 'seeing double', the queasy fear that the eye might 'take in' the extent of social infection and its bleeding off the edges of the screen right up to us. If a zombie does ever get to the top floors it scans only its own level. Bound to the ground, often dragging a leg as if still chained, the zombie has bitten out panoptic imagination and privileged separation. Turned on, it proceeds in straight lines across planes, a tunnel vision that it shares with those humans trying, fatally, to return to 'how things are'. 'What's Left Of Us' is evocative of this narrow and disconnected gaze that turns the panoptic and domineering gaze inwards, against those gazing.

There is an argument to be made for porosity in an apocalyptic landscape. In 'Pontypool' (2008), in which infection is communicated by speech rather than bite, it is only by maintaining a two-way spoken communication (almost the whole movie is set within a talk radio station) that life can return. In 'What's Left' what mostly goes out of the home is bullets, while Axel and Jonathan's bringing a young, handsome, male corpse into the living room in 'El Desierto' only adds to the rot and suppressed aggression/desire that is already there; there is no real exchange. Symptomatic of the ruin of these survivors is not so much their subsequent maltreatment of this zombie – they use him as both a punchbag and a painting canvas – as their ignoring of him. Only after the failure of Jonathan's attempt to have Ana and Axel resolve their complex tangle of contempt and desire by sleeping together, which breaks down when their diegetic 'soundtrack' cuts out, does the zombie finally come back into frame; rescuing the movie from the idea that the malevolent gaze within the house might be a residue of cheated love. Axel completes a 'dare', staring directly into the zombie's eyes; aghast at what he does or does not recognise there. The re-animated youth is indifferent to all this performing; his is a body exclusively for flesh. Despite his apparently moody indifference to the survivors' displays, he is always ready to snap his jaws at their hands and faces when they come too close. He will not perform, he will act.

Ana moves into the room where the zombie is chained. Then, with finality, she chooses him over the living men, his drive and fetid flesh over their life-saving and life-numbing organisation, his indifference over their scopophilic desires. She offers her wrist; he bites down into the deep riches of her flesh. Once the surface is burst and her blood and the zombie's infection have mixed, Ana chains herself in preparation for her change; completing her incarceration, freeing herself into the thickness of a zombie body and its indifference to the pain of being a surface endlessly gazed upon.

> *Spring this trap. Wander your city, slipping between its malevolent gazes. Locate and avoid the sweep of CCTV cameras. Work your way around security guards' fields of vision. Walk invisible; take routes that discourage admiring or hostile looks, possessing and defining stares. Do not dress any differently, up or down, from what you usually wear; the Romero zombie is a democratic and ordinary figure. No one*

costumes for reanimation. Instead, find ways of controlling the malevolent gaze by evading or rebuffing it, slipping beyond it, challenging it, wandering in the shadows and behind the scenes when you want, hiding in plain sight when you choose. Let performance fall away and walk for yourself and your pleasure alone. Not unwary and unaware, but using your sensitivity to the many gazes, and to the many baited stages and platforms of the city, to 'make your own way'.

4/ canon to the right of us, canon to the left

'What's Left Of Us' is one of a number of living dead products – others might include 'Pontypool', 'Defoe', 'La Horde' – that have moved the Romero mythos on in terms of political and cultural complexity. Of course, there has to be something coherent in the first place to be moved on from. I would claim that there is; that within the multiple unevenness and inconsistencies of the living dead sub-genre, each of them meaningful in themselves, there is a resilient and consistent Romero strain that runs through products from comics like Robert Kirkman's 'The Walking Dead' and 'Marvel Zombies' to Steve Niles' 'Batman: Gotham County Line', through novels like those by Luke Duffy, Gary McMahon, Colson Whitehead and David Wellington and in TV series like 'In The Flesh' and Charlie Brooker's 'Dead Set'.

The genealogy of this mythos runs forwards and backwards. For example, those apparently originary mall scenes from Romero's 'Dawn of the Dead' were prefigured in scenes, filmed five years earlier, of the dead swarming in a supermarket in 'Messiah of Evil' (1973). Or the apparently unique self-reflexivity of 'Pontypool' prefigured in the zombie audio drama 'The Peoria Plague' produced in 1972 by local radio station WSWT. The same goes for the sub-sub-genre's meaning; Roger Luckhurst's assertion that "it was only retrospectively, then, that 'Night' became a zombie film" (p.138) is perhaps even more acute than he realises. Just as there is a thickness and consistency running through the body of the Romero monster, so the same applies to its corpus of product. It changes slowly, but it changes across the whole field. In form and content it resists the acceleration and fluidity of hypermodernity, yet not with stasis but with a recalcitrant entanglement of its multiple figures. Watch two Romeroesque movies and it is not so hard to convince yourself that 'they are all the same', but watch twenty and you will grasp how the variations in individual films are not departures from an orthodoxy, but the tweaking of an entire field.

A recognisably Romeroesque corporeality and uncanny ambience is evident in films as different as 'The Living Dead at the Manchester

Morgue'/'Non Si Deve Profanare Il Sono Dei Morti' (1974),' The Return of the Living Dead' (1985), the movie-within-a-movie in 'Kitsutsuki To Ame', (2011), 'Cockneys vs Zombies' (2012), 'Before Dawn' (2013) 'Les Revenants' (2004) and 'What's Left Of Us'. The living dead young man in this last film is just as stolid and taciturn as any of the ghouls from the original 'Night' and the movie's ambience is every bit as sincere and grimly restrained (within the ranges of what is possible in a cannibalistic sub-genre) as anything by Romero. Unevenness in technical competence, aesthetic choice and even intention (as I will observe in relation to 'Colin') do little to destabilise the canon's coherence.

More interesting though is why there is coherence.

Partly, it is the effect of a radical yet ambiguous 'breaking-from' that Romero and his fellow film makers effected in 1968. The ambiguity of this process is best expressed by the German word *aufheben*, meaning both to abolish and also to preserve and raise to another level at the same time. In the case of the makers of 'Night' their *aufhebung* is a disconnection and sublimation of something which they do not acknowledge is there to be broken from: the colonial zombie. Instead, the model monster from which they explicitly borrow and depart is the virus-bearing vampire of Richard Matheson's novel *I Am Legend*, already adapted to film in 'The Last Man on Earth' (1964). To avoid making too obvious a copy, Romero and his fellow filmmakers shifted incrementally away from this vampire to a flesh-eating ghoul, a cannibal corpse, re-animated by an alien pollutant or radiation effect arriving on Earth by crashed satellite. Despite the rather narrow range of influences, the makers of 'Night' contrived to locate their 'new' monsters somewhere among the conflation made by 1950s' US pulp comics of 1920s' and 1930s' pseudo-ethnographies and Hollywood voodoo, emerging themes of post-war normotic personality and 'organisation men', and the fascination-horror of Nazi conformities and atrocities.

In his *Zombies: a cultural history*, Roger Luckhurst describes how these pulps prefigured key characteristics of the Romero monster, particularly its reflexivity and its "*massification* of death" (p.114), the realisation of the "potential multiplicity [of] the post-Frankenstein monster" (p.53, Halberstam). Luckhurst cites as exemplary of this process, the 1939 comic story 'While Zombies Walked' in which the narrator comes to realise that plantation workers who behave "like soldiers suffering from shell-shock" are in fact zombies not as a result of any narrative revelation, but through a pop-cultural daydream: "a confusion of mental images from a book on jungle rites – a paragraph from a voodoo thriller – scenes from one or two fantastic motion pictures" (quoted, pp.64-65). Given such reflexivity, long pre-dating Romero's genre making and bending, a hopeful search for an authentic and agentive origin in the material histories of slave revolt seems largely beside the point (though often detaining the reader through early sections of books such as Luckhurst's and Jennifer Rutherford's). And reactionary, too; it is no accident that white leftists first associated voodoo and zombies with resistance, while black anti-colonialists tended to see them as part of a discourse of repression and superstitious deception.

Suggestions that "the past returns in a new mutation... Romero conceived of this first modern zombie film as a return to the original zombies of Haiti" (p.36, Rutherford) would have more of a point if there were such a thing as "original zombies of Haiti", and if Romero had been able to achieve his early plans for a living dead trilogy which would end with "zombies who are operative... a return to what the zombie was in the beginning: Lugosi always lived in a castle while the zombies went out to pick sugar cane" (pp.47-48, Romero & Williams). But he did not, and the Romero monster retained its distinctive coherence and distance from the reactionary colonial zombie despite the first plans of its creator. So what it distances itself from is not a history of slavery and colonialism, their resonances are there, but from a 'zombie' that was always a production within fictional texts, inventive travel writing and pseudo-ethnography tangled together and then re-woven in reference to each other.

For me, any remaining confidence in the usefulness of seeking in Haiti's history or in the narrative genealogy of voodoo for certainty in the meaning of the Romero monster crumbled when I came across a Christmas ghost story of 1893. Published in a small regional paper in the West of England, the text contains a description of a "room full of animated corpses" that is remarkably consistent with the conventions and appearances of the Romero living dead: "yellow and blue faces, sunken mouths, dull half-closed eyes... the women and men assembled surrounded the undertaker... one poor fellow who carried his head... buried... in that fashion through a mistake in the measurement... a small skeleton pushed his way through the crowd... His skull smiled... bits of light green and red cloth, and old linen, hung here and there about him, as upon a pole... tottered, fell and went to pieces" (pp.30-32, Gray). Knowingly or not, Romero's limited precedents contained multiple elements from across times and cultures, which 'Night' then assembled, deleted and reanimated in an almost unrecognisable form; a classic palimpsest.

What gives the Romero zombie coherence, despite this complex contriving, is that it eschews any veiled representation of a subversive figure from a real world (whether slave or worker or lifeless 'organisation man') in favour of a transformation (*aufheben*) of materials whose anachronistic and anodyne qualities it cancels out and then returns as vitally horrific to 1968. This coherence comes neither from historical roots nor adherence to genre-tradition, but arrives by the way that it conserves as it traduces a set of parlous fictions which it fails to acknowledge even as it transforms them. The resilience of this coherence lies in the evolving sub-genre's resistance to precise categorisation and its continuing to mash up purloined, recycled and self-referenced materials; the surface features of one film returning as the hidden properties of another. Evan Calder Williams has proposed that this proclivity of the living dead sub-genre to simultaneously transgress and maintain is there from the start, present in the way that imaginary boundaries and precedents are in a paradoxical state from the beginning, with Romero "establish[ing] the rules of the genre... [while] already screwing around with those very rules". Williams identifies the way that 'Night' ignores and cancels a tradition while at the same moment re-inventing it: "[it] 'misreads' source material that was never there" (p.76).

Starting with J. R. Bookwalter ('The Dead Next Door'), many of the makers of zombie films who followed Romero began as fans; their enthusiasm for the sub-genre often leads them to simultaneously copy, refine and (knowingly and unknowingly) traduce it. The fine interweavings of sources and influences by writers and directors, under conditions of the accelerating exchange of images and commodities in a globalised economy, means that, in some sense, each zombie artefact produced contains the essence of the others. So, although many people are unlikely to have seen more than a few of the products cited here, whatever each of us has encountered is mythos enough for our purposes. Neither completionism nor purity is helpful. For not only does the post-Romero zombie retain its original instability of essence, but, at the same time, an uneasy fundamentality is crucial to its resilience.

This destructive, subversive and paradoxical foundation was explicitly discussed among the crew during the filming of 'Night' in 1967: "the disintegration of the family unit, the idea of revolution and that stuff" (p.26, Hervey). Ever since when, critics and fans and other movie makers have drawn attention to the resonance and convenience of the zombie as a metaphor for 'dead labour' and the exploitation, repression and imprinting of slave, worker and consumer. All pretty obvious stuff, and, as Evan Calder Williams points out, not an interpretation at all but simply what happens in the movies. Williams goes much further in genuine analysis, and has it about right: what powers the mythos is an expression of life in surplus, of the violence underlying everyday life, of the potential for collectivity to threaten everything else, and the revelation within the apocalypse of "how real abstractions work on real bodies... a way to model and map what happens when seemingly spectral shifts in the global architecture of a totality (capitalism), which cannot be traced to any one cause or agent, touch earth and produce real consequences" (p.80). It is for these reasons that taking close and obsessive notice of the likes of 'Les Revenants' or 'La Horde' (and, sometimes, even the naff and reactionary products of the Romero mythos) repays our attention, for each simultaneously and unevenly embodies and represents those "spectral shifts in the global architecture" and their real world consequences. It is for those same reasons that I am writing this book.

While I have become increasingly less impressed by my own argument that the yarn about a satellite in the original 'Night' means little and can be passed off as a MacGuffin (pp.131-2, Smith, 2012), I am still confident that it does not illuminate the zombies' behaviour within a viewing of the film. To all appearances these monsters are not ciphers for communism, nor are they radiated or possessed. They rise and walk because that is what they do, they are part of the pattern of the movie rather than a pattern external to it. Complementary to the movie's general landscape of dread, in the sense of causeless anxiety or fear, the living dead are part of a causeless, endless and pointless mission, rendering them poignant as well as scary; they are versions of us and our coming redundancy.

However, the Romero canon is a long way from establishing a monopoly of the living dead. It is barely hegemonic, with multiple artefacts appearing under zombie or living dead titles that are sharply at odds with the principles of the Romero canon. For example, in Europe's most significant early response to Romero, rather than being stripped away, the cause of the cannibalistic mission of its monsters is made explicit and historical. Amando de Ossorio's 'Blind Dead' movies (1971-5) feature an elite male group of deceased Templar Knights. These constitute not an alternative population of wanderers, traversing America in straight lines, or meandering inquisitively about places like 'place hackers' or 'dérivistes' in abandoned urban landscapes, but a malevolent squad, emerging from European ruins to descend on their victims as punishment for their neuroses, modernity, vulnerability and marginalised identities.

In contrast, the Romero mythos has a female zombie that is as much a consuming dead commodity as the male. She is equally freed from the social conventions of consumption. She walks at liberty through daunting urban terrains and empty rural landscapes that her counterpart in the cinema audience might steer clear off. So when the zombie is defined male, as with the Templar dead, it is an addition to repression; a supernatural cop ready to punish the unproductive and the non-reproductive. In comparison to this regressive violence, the Romero zombie's hungry gaze and meandering predation are much closer to the ambiguous qualities of 'benevolent' tailing and stalking in art actions like Vito Acconci's 'Following Piece' (1969) or Sophie Calle's 'Suite Venitienne' (1980) where unknowing strangers are followed and documented by artists who sought to surrender their volition to the objects of their gazes.

When Italian director Lucio Fulci responded to the success in European movie theatres of Romero's 'Dawn of the Dead' with an unofficial sequel, 'Zombi 2' (1979), the initially Romero-like opening scenes in New York harbour were followed by the lumbering entrance of History: cinema history. "Less an imitation Romero than a bloodier return to the zombie 'B' pictures of the 1940s" (p.190, Newman); reactionary Hollywood voodoo rose again. This morbid Past is far from at rest, but has repeatedly shown itself ready and armed with threadbare properties – portals, past indiscretions and empty houses – to return in movies like 'The Zombie Chronicles' (2001) or Uwe Boll's 'House of the Dead' (2003), repeating its punishment of the modern (in Boll's case, ravers) and its caricatures of history ('Chronicles' not defaming the Templars this time, but putting the US entanglement in Vietnam down to bad drill).

> Attend 'living history' events, fancy dress processions and historical reconstructions of the battle of wherever or the coronation of whatshername as the historic dead. Go as a heroine long since in her grave and rotted, or the reanimated remains of the victims and losers of colonial discovery: Tasmans perhaps. You might make-up heavily de-composed and disrupt the pageant through the general disgust at your having noticed that these events are all about the deceased, or maybe just sufficiently blue in the face to provoke the question of time passing.

A similarly reactionary invocation of a malleable yet universal Past held back the development of walking arts for a while, tying it to long distance extreme walking, to solo, male and heroic practice, and to dominant images of nature and the wild that removed it from urban sites and made it inaccessible to most people. A morbid universality pervaded the work of some of the most influential European walking artists whose work emerged during the 1960s and 1970s and it has either defined, or at least prefaced, any understanding of walking arts ever since. This is personified in the somewhat elusive figure of Richard Long who has repeatedly privileged "places where nothing seems to have broken the connection to the ancient past" (p.272, Solnit).

In the art of walkers like Long or Hamish Fulton, or at least in its residue, the walking body disappears. Instead the task attempted is figured in graphics of miles walked, of starting and finishing points, as if these were the most significant, and a refusal to let anyone else into the art ("which is the walk"). This modernist elitism would be challenged around the cusp of the 21st century by situationist-inspired walkers such as Drew Mulholland, Anna Best and Jim Colquhoun for whom the texts of Iain Sinclair and the activities of occult psychogeographers seem to have served as a bridging device to earlier disruptions. They often involved others, sometimes in group walking, and they shared details and representations of their walks, offering affects and tips and provocations for others to draw on. They prefigured and helped to define the explosion of walking arts that then took place in the decade that followed: mostly sociable, located, relational, accessible, playful, radical.

Yet even these walkers often listed their genealogies as if nothing had changed since the 1970s. Many (partly due to the popularity of Rebecca Solnit's *Wanderlust'*) located their work as extensions of, or responses to, the European and North American Romantic traditions of rural walking, of George Borrow, the Wordsworths, Coleridge and Henry David Thoreau. It is no accident that when Francesco Careri, one of the founders of Rome-based ambulatory-activist-architect group Stalker, came to review the history of walking arts in *Walkscapes* (2002) he emphasises trajectories and the transitory built environment of nomadism rather than make textual monuments to the literary luminaries of Romanticism. As an account of walking as art and activism, *Walkscapes* is a useful and combative companion to Solnit's *Wanderlust*. In Careri's historiography on the hoof, the wandering zombie would not appear as an anomaly, but as an every-body, an ambulatory menhir, a trajectory in trajectory that continues to move despite its thingness, a reminder that there is meandering in its very decay.

As a young movement, with a trailing heritage, the new walking arts quickly stumbled on the Dadaist paradox: having abolished 'art' what was it that they were making? The Dadaists had deambulated and led tours to derelict sites, while Surrealists and International Lettristes had archived urban anomalies and derelictions, floating them free from their accepted significance, following the Symbolists in detaching poetry from its objective correlatives and reassembling the fragments, amputating the city's stories about itself from their historical past. The first Lettristes went so far as to detach themselves even from the alphabets in which these histories were recorded. One problem that the walking arts has yet to solve is how to narrate this part of its tradition, of detachment, without closing the wound; how to preserve the independence of the fragments for their rearrangement (what situationists call 'détournement') in a future. The model of the Romero zombie is encouraging.

By distancing his zombies from explanation (although in 'Day of the Dead' – there is always an exception to zombie rules – a character does briefly speculate on a moral origin to the crisis) Romero gives us no who, where or when to blame but ourselves right here and right now. There is no displacement of action to interpretation or getting an excuse in early in the form of probabilities and strategic speculation. Romero puts no distance between us and the dead walking. They are us. In 'The Walking Dead', Rick is given the secret that all humans, not just the bitten, will reanimate when they die. Living and dead walk towards the same future, as bound together as the world and its humans in the narrative of 'the Anthropocene'. It is always a mistake in a Romero movie to resort to the bunker, because, in zombieland as in everyday life, separation is the problem not the solution.

The Romero zombie claws its way up towards time not through an ancient landscape, but out of an urban and popular dereliction, the failure of modernism and a panic-room full of contemporary ideology. This is the reversal of de Ossorio's embodied History on the hunt for scapegoats. De Ossorio's Templar zombies are agents of a bogus resilience. They do not rearrange ruins, but return to them after their predations on the weak, as if both they and their ruins could never be changed.

Romero zombies and situationist 'dérivistes' have no legitimating starting points and no final destinations to reach; they follow the atmospheres, dislocated from the everyday functioning of the city and its decision-making, their shambling and chaotic walking reveal flows and barriers that are usually invisible and unmarked gaps in the fabric that are otherwise ignored. Just as the living dead have an unnerving ability to fold time, suddenly and without warning becoming very close, 'dérivistes' can slow themselves to give attention to the fine texture of the city and then accelerate to a pace at which they become sensitive to sudden changes in ambience and to the flows of images, things and organisms as they move from one space to the next.

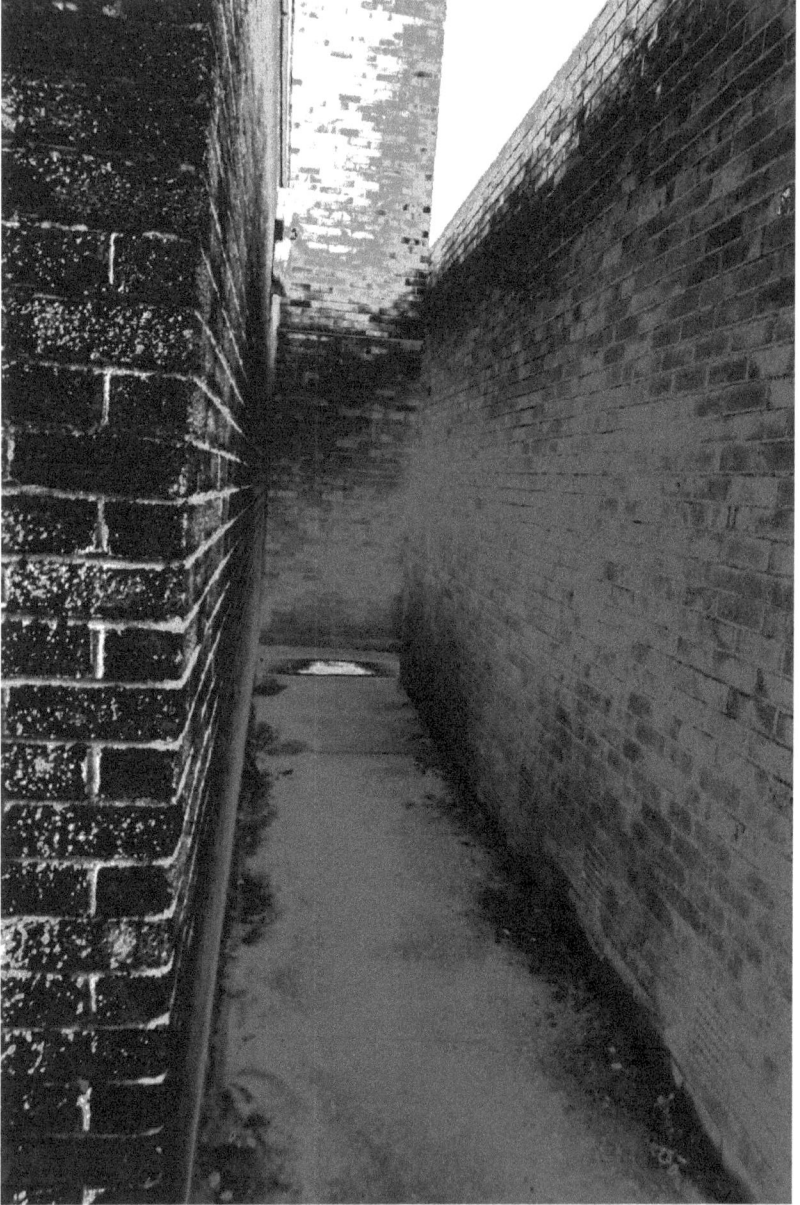

5/ fear and feeling

To walk as a survivor of an apocalypse, aware of the potentials and affordances of space, is not a mathematical exercise; calculating areas, distances and accelerations may help you, but only a little. Maps may even throw up a layer of representation that hides what the real terrain is capable of.

> *Walking survivor-aware is mostly about developing your sensitivity to ambience, to the 'feel' of space, trusting to your gut feeling, your first instinct, hypersensitising yourself to those genii of spacetime that all your sensual computations compress and then disperse in the miasma of a place's 'atmosphere'. Teach yourself to pinpoint the details, signs, texture and meanings of a place – not as a narrative or a thesis, but as a series of sensual flashes – and then draw them in and mix them up with your own preoccupations and intuitions. In the flows and fluctuations of these sparkling micro-particles of emotional information you will feel a mood or swell develop, of which you are a part; this will give you the first hint of a complex meaning and significance of a locus.*
>
> *Walk its approximate shape into your memory; store it, story it, and draw upon it later.*

This kind of immediate sensitivity to ambience comes before either reflection or analysis. Nevertheless, it is just as coherent, repeatable and identifiable.

> *Stop. Listen. Count how many different birdsongs. Count how many different motors. Count how many different kinds of whistle. Look carefully around you, slowly turning your head; then turn your body through 360 degrees. List the kinds of red, the various intensities of mesh, the numbers of tendrils or loose*

threads or consonants. Walk to another space and this time forget about such mechanics. Just let a general sense (don't try to think it into words) wash over you, or creep up on you, or hammer at you; each space will impose its ambience in different ways. Sharp, foggy, melancholic, agitated; each space will have an ambience.

In your 'heart', in the hairs on your arm, in the drying and moistening of your mouth, feel for anxieties about the city's invisible orders (what it knows about you, what it holds of yours, what it might prosecute against you); walking in the twilight find a view to a horizon and imagine the shapes of that power silhouetted against the living dead landscape.

Visit different places of the same genus (a selection of halls, or gardens, or waste grounds, or betting shops, or roadsides); don't stay more than a minute or so, but train yourself to absorb impressions in that time. Don't impose stories; let the characters and events come to you out of the ambience.

By playing scenes from the living dead mythos in your head as you traverse the city, cultivate a low level paranoia. You will develop super-sensitivity to certain architectural shapings, urban textures, texts, flows and codes. By reversing the principle of Occam's Razor (the simplest explanation is always the most likely) and over-interpreting, a living corpse around each corner, you will see an imaginary potential everywhere, you will bathe everything in possibilities. Every object will conceal a second object. You do not even need to imagine any particular scenario; you are not trying to frighten yourself, but make yourself sensitive to the locale by the fiction of a threat with no real cause. Fear without a cause is what the philosopher Søren Kierkegaard called 'dread', it's a particularly useful feeling because it works like a terrier hunting down the ideological origins of fears in the tunnels of one's feelings.

This is what the situationists called 'psychogeography'; emotional information gathered by setting oneself at the mercy of a place; testing a place against the psychological effect it has on its traversers, which requires a certain self-knowledge and attention to feelings on the part of the psychogeographer. In the occult variant of psychogeography, the ambience, the atmosphere of the place (its *genius loci*), is taken for a real and material thing rather than simply the traverser's subjective responses to it: this is comparable to how Asgar Jorn takes spatial geometry and refutes its ideal, universal and abstract qualities, instead treating it as a physical practice for creating 'situations' that are measured as they are made from "the point of view of the joyrider of time rather than that of the detective who contemplates the stretched, squeezed, or folded remains after the event" (p.17, Wark). Objectified and materialised, yet retaining their subjective measurement in this way, a supernatural atmosphere functions as a kind of useful subtraction from (and abstraction of) the place, upsetting the idea of a place as somewhere 'always-already' captured in signs and symbols; freeing it from a purely functional role in the social spectacle, investing it with some agency and independence, liberated, temporarily, from its representations.

Of course, such an agency can swiftly return as spectacle and representation in the form of esoteric texts and fictions. Nevertheless, though occult and literary psychogeographers have littered obfuscations in literary form, it was they who kept the practice of psychogeography vibrant when materialist post-situationists were strangling it with unimaginative algorithms. By their privileging of something numinous (invisible, at least) they created a gap between the place and what can be represented of it. We do not have to be overly romantic about this numinous anti-matter; those forces favouring the powerful are just as active in the numinous as at a border crossing or within the text and visual codes of a news broadcast. Nevertheless, 'zombie walking' can enter the gap that occult psychogeography leaves as the opposite of the 'always ready' of the spectacle; something like the 'always unprepared' of places, affordant to what the anti-psychiatrists and neo-vitalist theorists Gilles Deleuze and Felix Guattari called "writ[ing] at n-1 dimensions", which is the liberating of a multiplicity from its ruling force by freeing its parts from its commanding organism. In our case that ruling force is the spectacle and the parts we are liberating are images, codes and things (including human beings), its most powerful commanding organism is the meme of self and from that the parts we are liberating are memories, associations, affects and visions of the future.

In order to effect such a liberation from self, 'zombie walking' seeks to break from at least part of the tradition of walking arts, ditching the passive and haughty part of the legacy of "the flâneur as a scholar of the street" and replacing his (sic) cool disengagement with an almost-overwhelmed immersion, emphasising and appropriating a predatory streak already present in the flâneurs hanging around the Parisian arcades (precursors to Romero's mall): "wandering souls who go looking for a body… enter[ing]… into each man's personality" (p.20, Baudelaire). The disrupted pedestrian is an appetite-driven wanderer, a window-shopper who resists the commodity itself. Emphasising the physical, the haptic and the contemplative rather than the intellectual and the analytical, 'zombie walking' takes from its models – of a terrified yet controlled survivor and a living-dead body blasphemously unencumbered by a soul – a greedily moving in and out of sociability rather than above it, a switching voraciously and ambiguously from moment to moment between "surfacing and disappearing in the crowd" (p.1, Fincham, McGuinness & Murray).

To walk with the reanimated corpse as your model is not about reinterpreting the real world as a cannibal movie. Nor is it about categorising real-world events in terms of apocalyptic fiction as happened with the so called 'bath salts' attack in Miami in 2012 when an African-American man suffering a psychotic episode was shot dead by police after biting off parts of a victim's face.

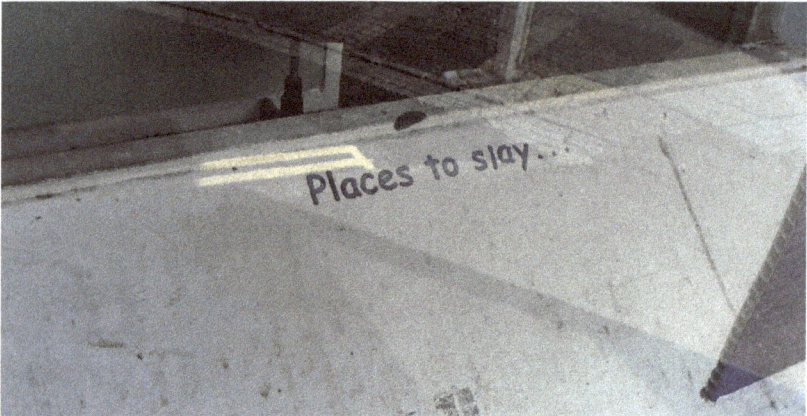

"Some of them shambled about unsettlingly… Others were as ravenous [as] rabid predators, repugnantly ripe to rip out some poor regardless patron's rank guts" (p.248, Marcelo) – these reflections of a horror fan on his fellow citizens out Christmas shopping demonstrate how quickly what I am proposing here, put to work in a bad way, can be turned into a discourse of normatising cynicism. That is not what using the corpse model is about;

done correctly it is you that takes on the role of the despised and repugnant, the compromised and helplessly driven outlaw.

But why walk with a corpse as model? On the one hand, it can work as a kind of shadow. A composting and re-composing of denigrated parts of ourselves. On the other, it serves as an odd mimicry, a kind of unflashy reflection, a default against which to compare anything, a touch-thing by which to re-site ourselves socially and politically. I may not be right about either quality, you must decide that, but my reason for believing that something unites them is very simple: we must walk as what we fear.

The philosopher, Hans Jonas, advocated a 'hermeneutics of fear', partly as a way to get our anxieties to fuel our understandings. On the face of it, it seems the perfect philosophy for an intelligent understanding of horror. However, there is a problem with the rationale that Jonas proposed. He asserted that only our fear of the extinction of humanity and the loss of our unique consciousness will prevent the actual loss of either. Unfortunately, we have *already* feared all that and we are still willing to gamble the future against a slim chance that things may turn out 'all right' in the end. Despair, which can be energised by pessimism about the behaviour of others, is a far better basis for agency and understanding, rather than fear, which pessimism only makes more frozen and freezing. And some fears feed no hermeneutics at all: they are felt by those who 'know' the city, who are ignorant from the inside, who study the newspaper reports and follow the crime programmes, who perceive crime levels to be far higher than they actually are, creating a gap that is a reactor of ideological power; inverting the imaginary-predator hermeneutics for a hermeneutics of imaginary predators. This is an inversion of dread and is anterior to withdrawal rather than freedom, all very different from the modernist city and 'shock of the new'. Instead, this is the hermeneutics of the bunker, the morals of the panic room. Those who indulge it are a danger to themselves and everyone else in dangerous times. In a bible for such uncreative paranoia (controlled not by the experience, but by other manipulators), *20th Century City & Urban Survival*, the anonymous author gives chilling vent to these kinds of imaginary fears (rather than fears of the imaginary), but then gives the game away: "In city and suburbia everyone is out to fleece you in one way or another, and everyone is vulnerable". Here it is then; the ideology laid out and self-anatomised for all to see: the dark urban night in which *everyone* is sheep and *everyone* is wolf, each one of us simultaneously victim and serial killer, attacked and attacker – we are doing this to ourselves! By zombie walking, stepping on both sides of these binaries – "the walking dead – both victim and perpetrator" (p.73, Rutherford) – as living living and living dead, as sheep and wolf, we can live *with* all these fears. Even in this most negative of fear-hermeneutics there lurks 'Life' and hybridity in all their wonderful excess. For anxiety and desire can walk creatively together in the city; otherwise, after a while, nothing walks at all.

So, it is not the outright avoidance or rejection of fear that helps; rather it is our choosing what we take as the model for what we fear. It is by melding what we feel with what we desire. That which on the surface makes no sense at all is what will work for us. This is what I mean by a reparative agency of despair. By taking a predatory pleasure in the future, by making use of what we fear and what threatens us (even though we cannot control them), and by standing against any loss of aggregate pleasure now, we change parameters. By giving respectability to such 'irresponsibility' it becomes possible to continue with the planet, not by good deeds and guilty feelings, but by ambiguous deeds, by feeding the liberating loneliness and anonymity of the city that sparks change: "the ethico-political misery of our epoch whose ultimate mobilising motif is the mistrust of virtue" (p.xxxix, Žižek, 2008). Fear and gratification must go together, or, after a while, nothing goes at all. Hypocrisy is the glue that binds them; it and living in obscurity are uneasy keys to getting by and doing good in this slow apocalypse. Despairing of action, yet still acting in despair. Local indulgence and global asceticism (combining 'do as I say and not as I do' with the operating principles of zombieland) will not save the world any more than the present global regime, but they can serve as twists in a collective slowing down and an entangled decline into despairing grace. Global indulgence and an unevenly successful and evenly marginalising advocacy for private asceticism – in other words what we have now – only make things worse. 'Act locally, think globally' is no more appropriate a slogan for the Anthropocene than 'keep calm and carry on'. And before you object to statist interventions at global level, consider what a nightmare the principles in the first part of this paragraph – pleasure, gratification, irresponsibility – might invoke without communal and legal protection affording 'freedom from' as well as 'freedom to'?

By walking, both fearful and attracted, respecting people's fears despite your distrust of their cause, you combine wanting and wariness and make possible, at least for yourself, sudden shiftings across the plane of ideology, during which first attraction and then discipline can assert themselves; the shocks of the new followed by their shepherding into old folds, allowing you to stake new claims to, and make new rearrangements of, existing ideas. Paranoia is the centralising element for this kind of sudden state-change.

Limited paranoia gives you binocular vision, putting you simultaneously inside the secret operations of society and outside as one of the oppressed; a super-positioned sensitivity to 'what is really going on' that can help you locate and describe the movement of the crucial imaginary machine, the ideological orrery which shows the exact mechanics of the dominance of symbols, images and stories. Limitation is crucial; an operation like those of Dumézil's one-eyed magician emperor, cited by critical theorists Deleuze and Guattari as ruling by "capture, bonds, knots, and nets" (pp.468-9). The theorists saw both the sovereign and those ruled by him as produced incomplete: "the state apparatus makes the mutilation, and even death, come first. It needs them preaccomplished... crippled and zombielike" (p.470); what I am proposing in despair is by reversing sovereignty, but retaining and deploying its limitation upon the psyche, to turn death and injury into a Life constituted of and maintained by the landscape, the symbols at work in it, and the spring of your body that turns it. By momentarily revealing alignments in its workings this orrery shows you when and where you can operate asymmetrically, taking advantage of the sudden effectiveness of a statement here, of a gesture there, to shift giant ideological structures with simple interventions. This orrery is accessible to anyone willing to walk as both living-living and living-dead, to set themselves at the mercy of the terrain, and to sensitize themselves to the attitudes and inclinations of a post-apocalyptic world that has been reverse-engineered to now.

> *One of your eyes is involved in a conspiracy. What you see, at least part of the time, is not reality but a distortion of it created by the conspiring eye in order to discredit the other. Do not try to end this happy event; rather, take advantage of this competition – between one dead eye, and one living – in order to see in multiple ways, testing the confabulations of your eyes against conspiracies of real matter out there beyond the sclera.*

This is the next step for Barbra, the physical embodiment to which this chapter of fancy has been building itself up: rather than walking as an imaginary survivor, you can begin to add to your walk certain elements from the walk of the living dead themselves.

6/ the zombie-human: peacefully violent, individual and collective

There is a discussion around the zombie apocalypse which has nothing to do with prisons, bunkers or cabins and does not anticipate a threat that inevitably comes from within the embattled community, but is all about entangling a 'within' with a 'without', in both self-reflection and social relations. It is from here that a communal strength can come.

Margaret Killjoy warns that "if you want to survive you should not go run and hide in your little isolated cabin by yourself or with five of your friends... this sort of cowardice, this individualistic gusto... arguably got us into this trouble in the first place" ('How to survive the collapse of civilisation', Dodgem Logic #5). Killjoy suggests fighting back against fascistic militarisation and "kickstarting a permacultured agriculture to feed people". A model for such collective and non-hierarchical resistance lies not only in the generosity of the living, but in the radicalism of the recently re-animated dead, the Cadaver Spring, in the refusing to live as the living have always done, in the apocalyptic overturning of dynamic patterns in deep machine-organisms, disrupting swarm species in stock markets, the urban drift from East to West and 'how things are'.

The zombie infection is not that dissimilar to the idea of the 'human strike', the refusal, like that of Herman Melville's character 'Barnaby', to participate in the everyday, especially in production and consumption. To anti-live and un-survive on an occasional ginger biscuit. Lee Miller has evoked a "co-operative community" of the living dead, with their sense of "the importance of community... One zombie will never hide behind another zombie when the shooting starts... [They] set aside selfish needs, and instead appear to serve a collective need, however accidental that might be" (p.197).

Ann Deslandes and Kristian Adamson call this "zombie solidarity". They take the image of the human zombie "duped... half living... forced through the drudgery of the bureaucratic and corporate process" and refine it to describe "those who refuse to turn on each other, refuse to take the flesh of their colleagues, those that disrupt and refuse the benefits of a world they find... distasteful" (p.78). If we look again at the first 'Dawn' movie, we'll see that the zombies there are not only "far from being the ideal consumer subject... a nightmarish subject that fails to be interpellated by the economic discourses of consumer spaces" but also "achieved two things that the living couldn't: they managed to refrain from turning on each other and they resisted, through disinterest, the privilege and comforts of the mall" (pp.71, 78).

Gather together a few friends and explore the city in 'zombie solidarity'. This is a complex practice, a swarming by ones, very different to that first walking as 'Barbra', particularly given the infected notion of 'exploration', requiring you to stay mindful of its colonialist undertone. This is no zoology of the streets.

You need time, and a quiet space where you can practice some collective zombie figures together before you set out into public spaces. That might be a room you can use, or a space in a park that is not too busy. Begin by sharing your ideas about zombies, discuss some of the ideas from this book, 'zombie solidarity', the cooperativeness of the living dead and how their seeking of flesh can be interpreted as expressions of ordinary but repressed human desires suddenly released from social controls like convention, competition, property and so on.

In your space you can begin to make a benign 'living dead dance' by stitching together different zombie moves and modes of interaction that you can glean from zombie products; adapting them away from flesh-seeking and towards a pleasure in objects and spaces. Make sure everyone understands that they will be moving with others, so even when they are trying to act instinctively and spontaneously they still need to look out for each other. And that although you'll be working up to using movements from zombie movies there is no violence in those movements.

Start the physical stuff by having a quick warm up, shaking out your limbs and gently stretching muscles.

Then all walk around your space – you might need to make some limits if you are outside (your own temporary zombie pen).

Vary the pace – subtly, and then dramatically, fast and slow. All the time stay super-aware of each other, and avoid bumping into others. Once you have successfully walked at varying paces, interweaving with each other without accident, try, slowly at first, doing the same but now walking backwards. Begin gently, looking over your shoulder, only gradually speeding up. If you have a big group, you might want to try this first in smaller groups before everyone walks backwards together.

Now walk forwards again, with everyone trying to catch the eye of as many people as they can; acknowledging each connection with a nod, a smile or simple gesture.

Then everyone chooses someone else in the group and tries to follow them, trying not to let their subject know that they are being followed. The point here is that the follower lets themselves be controlled by the person they are following; this is not stalking, but surrendering control to an unknowing guide.

All walk again, but this time avoiding eye contact.

Then set the task of everyone trying to triangulate with two others (so as to make an equilateral triangle with them); again, if possible, this should be done without anyone becoming aware of who is walking in relation to who.

Then walk again, and this time practice stopping and starting simultaneously as a group with no signal from anyone, all feeling and waiting for the moment. Maybe try this in small groups and build up to the whole class together. Avoid the temptation to trigger others with subtle pre-emptings.

Then, with everyone in the space working alone, explore; waiting until you feel an inner pull or a push to a particular place or object in the space, surrendering to the attraction and letting yourselves be pulled by it; gently touching the object of your attention or savouring the feeling of being in that particularly part of the space. Once you feel your interest waning, start to look around the room again... letting yourself be drawn towards whatever attracts you next, whatever catches your eye. It may be a quality of light or a reflection, a particular material or texture, it may be a shadow, it may be the weight of an object. Allow yourselves to be pulled about the space by your own preferences and pleasures.

Now try the same exercise, but this time in one small group at a time. In each group each person should follow their attractions and pulls, but at the same time keep the group connected so that if any individual senses a stronger pull than their own on the part of another member of their group, that they then should follow that until they are pulled by a stronger one of their own or someone else's. The individuals should try to move as a group, but all the time responding to individual drives (their own and others'), feeling for the parts of the space and the things that the group are most attracted to, staying alert to any changes of pull in the group. Done right this models the uneven synthesis of individual urges with the common will of the horde.

Once the groups are moving confidently together, it will be time to learn some basic zombie movements and integrate them into the collective exploring. These movements are drawn from what I have identified as the 'Romero zombie'; you may want to add others from your own viewing and reading:

1/ milling (turning in small circles, focus turned in)

2/ herding (moving very close together, both slow and fast)

3/ trance (standing still, focus unfixed, perhaps with a gentle sway)

4/ suddenly emerging from hidden-ness

5/ holding and manipulating objects with an obsessive fixation upon them, as if they are dimly familiar.

6/ performing everyday actions as if only faintly and very crudely remembered.

7/ being led in a line by a 'Number 9' or a 'Big Daddy'.

8/ in a herd and being held at an obstacle (imagine a fence or a gate, perhaps) and then the sudden release as the barrier collapses and all move through in a sudden flood.

9/ as a group, suddenly targeting an object or point (not a person), heading there in a straight line (it may need someone to step outside of this and provide a focus by throwing, say, a shoe into the space); clustering with intense focus.

10/ clustering from different directions on a place or object, with intense pleasure, but careful not to obstruct others.

11/ spread out across the space (like zombies in fields), walking in the same direction, equally spaced apart.

12/ the traipse (as in 11, but closer together).

13/ grazing – slack-jawed, relaxed, ambling without direction and distractedly.

14/ any other moves you have recognised and want to add.

What is crucial is that no one tries to act as zombies or to improvise scenarios such as you might find in movies. This is not about performing characters, but about responding to attractions within oneself or recognised in others.

Try small group improvisations in the space, drawing on the palate of different moves, responding to stimuli in the space; its objects, shapes and textures. Each person should try to sense what the group is doing without choosing (unless you are leading a line [7 above]). The key principle (like in the zombie movies) is infection or transmission: if someone starts something, then allow it to infect you and take it on. First try with one group at a time, and then with all the groups, with care to ignore each other, steering into the gaps between the other groups.

In conventional naturalistic drama, the key to the dramatic dynamic is to discover what each character's unique objectives might be; both their immediate ones and their over-riding super-objective. In these exercises you are all driven by the same super-objective: attraction to the different elements of the space.

You should now be ready to try this in shared public spaces. First try it out in a relatively quiet space; later in major and busy ones. Be careful that you do not perform zombies – simply follow your own enjoyment of the new things that you are attracted to in the new spaces. As far as is possible do not interact with other members of the public, continue to respond to your strongest attractions to things and places. Be subtle in your collective movements; so that some passers-by will notice nothing unusual, while those who do detect something will not be able to quite identify what is 'wrong' or different. It is for these people, left to question what is 'normal' for them, to ponder what had changed in a familiar place, that the exercise may be most profound. If a member of the public does approach you, then stop and explain to them what you are doing and then, if appropriate, carry on.

You may feel more secure if one member of the group operates discreetly in the space as an 'outside eye', ready to intervene if necessary.

Once you are done, gather together and discuss the way you now feel about the spaces you moved in, what impact you have had, and what this has all done to you.

If you enjoyed it, do it again. Zombies are all about desire and repetition.

(I have discussed the use of this tactic in a teaching context in 'Using Zombies to Teach Theatre Students', 2016.)

7/ sex and the zombie

For scholar Simon Clark, George Romero's zombie is "an embodiment of... pleasure-seeking instincts... nothing less than a visual metaphor for the return of the repressed" (pp.198-199). In everyday life, these instincts are repeatedly and customarily torn from the bodies of the living by the restrictions of civilised behaviour, buried in compartmentalisations of what is acceptable, and neutralised by the hierarchies and power-legitimating of oppressive spaces that are given the patina of transgression: extremist training camps, sex parties, comedy shows, evangelical services. It takes something as excessive as the resurrection of the dead to metaphorically conceive of the return of instincts in their true liberating excess.

Max Brooks points out in *The Zombie Survival Guide* that it is a matter of common sense, given the weight of earth bearing down on dead bodies and coffin lids, that a cemetery is not a place where you are most in danger of zombie attack. Zombies, however, are not about common sense. They are about wild and uncivilised energies, capable of ripping through the surface of dead space; they have what Gilles Deleuze called "Life", a super-life that can overleap its vehicles and exceed both the organisation and logic of its materials – "it's organisms that die, not life" (p.143) – and the conventions of space. Hence "the 'living dead'... are in a way 'more alive than life itself,' having access to the life substance prior to its symbolic mortification" (p.131, Žižek, 1992); in other words, all the fancy geography and interpretation in this book will be to no avail unless we are willing to immerse our bodies, in the manner of the living dead, in the kinds of excessive energies that come before they can be represented in symbols, escaping representation no matter how monstrous its symbols might be.

> *Walk but don't think; just watch yourself. Watch what your body does. Watch what arises from it, what swirls within it. What does it want? What attracts it? Not what you think it should want but what it does want. What does it avoid? Not*

what you think you fear, but what does your body steer clear of? What rules frustrate it, what barriers restrain it? Don't analyse them, just watch.

The future is a projection of needs. Vitality is the capacity of self-organising systems to produce novel outcomes to meet those needs. An excessive 'Life' that does not require a non-material organising intelligence within the systems-in-us can never be wholly or forever frustrated. In the wasteland of despair, hope will come from an unexpected, uncontrollable, excited body.

Walk. Walk away from this book. Walk with your associations about zombies. Walk alone and spontaneously. Walk very ordinarily at first, very everyday, don't try yet to 'be' zombie. Walk without navigating, walk in a straight line through unpromising places until you find spaces where you can respond to excessive feelings without spectators. These may be waste grounds, empty alleys, edgelands, cloisters, they may be sheltered spaces just to one side of exposed or busy ones. Recently I walked for a week or so around Milton Keynes, a city constructed since the 1960s in southern England; I found that just to the side of many of the verges of its gridded road system were strips of wooded land where the undisturbed tall grasses told me that no one else had been in for weeks. Use such spaces to practice your pursuit of a Life that does not die when organisms die, a Life that keeps bubbling over, beyond structure, absurd, beyond the orders of the body. Follow and drag down the winds. Attack the sunset. Fill your mouth with dog barks. At a ruin absorb its crumble.

Later, in a crowd, pursue, discretely, energies that escape any single body. Reach out with your mind to the ripples, eddies and splashes that evade individual bodies. Absorb the patterns of pavement stains through your soles.

Simon Clark is more specific than I have been; the energy he is writing about is erotic. He turns the zombie narrative inside out. Instead of a catastrophe that causes the collapse of structured society, it is the "collapse of common authority... a void in civilisation's defences that sucks in the advancing horde of zombies" (p.200); loosed from the pressing matter of repression, erotic desires are free to roam during a zombie apocalypse, spreading like conversations, flesh entering flesh through the orifice of the mouth, indifferent to gender. It is at the mouth that Colin begins his predation, like a kiss, upon a body that seems to drop out of the sky; unholy manna. Sexuality planes out, unhindered by hierarchies and etiquettes; it is for once sincere, wrapped up in what it is, driven by its inner life, free of controls and rampant.

At least that goes for Romero zombies. Or, more precisely, for Clark's Freud-based interpretation of Romero's zombies. About both we should be guarded, particularly with respect to how applicable to anything else they might be: within Romero's canonical work there are few of the blatant objectifications of women that characterise many other examples of the sub-genre. The famously naked female corpse in 'Night' is filmed in uniformity with the other, clothed, bodies in the horde; a marker not only of gender, but of an everyday commonality in death that is more than skin deep; as Jennifer Rutherford writes of 'Night', "there is nothing eroticised about its violence" (p.61). However, it is not just on the porn-zombie margins or in unhappy appropriations by the mainstream that objectifications and abusive images appear.

'Thanatomorphose' (2012) is not strictly a zombie flick, though it might be characterised as a wholly unsentimental version of 'Maggie' (2015), without Arnie and Joely Richardson as supportive parents.

Perhaps paradoxically, this distance from the sub-genre enables it to isolate and narrate more uncompromisingly the rotting and infected body, the body giving birth to its dead self. At the end of the movie, what remains of the body of Laura, the central character, literally tears itself apart in its attempts to come into being dead. Despite the stripped down qualities of the movie, shot mostly in hyper-realistic mode with stretches of everydayness and ennui (punctuated by what might be nightmares, might be projected desires, might be events), the film overleaps itself when, absurdly, Laura's semifluid flesh and disarticulated bones conjure up an impossible final scream before her jaw literally drops to the floor.

The essentialism of the scene evokes special effects *tours-de-force* from Dracula's disintegration in sunlight to the crushing of the Terminator's metal skeleton. Far from a false move, 'Thanatomorphose's' concluding idiocy is ideologically impelled by the thesis of the movie; it is a final protest of what passes in the film for female desire, barely discouraged by the indifference and violence of partners and intensified by illness, decay and physical disarticulation. It is a crude filmic imagining of one part of the post-Freudian psychologist Jacques Lacan's often misinterpreted suggestion that there is no such thing as 'La Femme'. The director of 'Thanatamorphose', Éric Falardeau, has dramatised the idea that "woman is a symptom" (only able to enter the cultural economy as an object of men's desire), without Lacan's contextualising rejoinder that, unlike the Male, women "do not lend themselves to generalisation, not even phallocentric generalisation". 'Thanatomorphose' passes off 'Laura-as-symptom', a product of her oppression in a society of self-serving and indifferent men, as her general state, body, drive and identity; her illness and disintegration only exaggerating her desire for more of her symptom. Her offer, in her decomposed state, to fellate a disgusted male suitor, and her then stabbing him to death when he turns her down, is proposed as a marker of her essential and now exceptionally revealed female agency; a thinly veiled male fantasy object, demanding to be available even at the point of death.

The indie-zombie movie 'The Battery' (2012) repeats the problem, light-heartedly; another warning against approaching Simon Clark's sexual utopianism unwarily. In 'The Battery', which conforms to most of the tropes of the Romero mythos within the frame of a slacker road-movie, the symbolic, cross-gender ambiguity of the zombie proposed by Clark – part *vagina dentata* on legs, part stiff shambling erection – collapses. The key scene is a comic travesty of the sequence in Romero's original 'Dawn' where a generously bellied male bounces repeatedly against one of the outer doors of the Monroeville mall. In 'The Battery', however, it is a young female zombie who, in her attempts at predation, inadvertently presses her breasts repeatedly against the side window of a motor vehicle while the male survivor inside beats himself off. Any ambiguity around the female character's objectification, given shifting camera viewpoints and the comical-critical portrayal of the male character's sexual desperation, is resolved when ejaculation is both pre-empted and replaced by the blood showering from the woman's head as it is pulverised by gunfire from the masturbator's buddy. Repression is piled upon repression upon repression upon repression; and the woman (listed in the end credits as FRESH ZOMBIE SLUT) is obliterated, as if her objectification were her own fault.

These are cautionary moments. The idea that a catastrophe's release of sexual energy will assume ideal forms is a deeply unwise one: the zombie mythos is "not a utopic fantasy in which man is liberated from the subject/object conundrum, nor is it a riotous celebration of the apocalypse that would ensue if humanity were able to get free of the subject/object bind" (unpaginated, Lauro & Embry). There would be nothing good about a real zombie apocalypse; it would simply fulfil shock capitalism's revolutionary fantasies of starting all over again from scratch (think Pol Pot). While the narrative of survivors moving through a transformed and empty space, its revenge on the neo-liberal world ("the night of the crash... more people than just me were mentally picturing libertarian fantasies of well-dressed, well-nourished human beings walking the world's streets like zombies trying to buy gasoline... except money no longer works" [unpaginated, Baser *et al*]), with its fantasies of 'free shopping' and small, survivalist utopian mini-communities may have a radical style, in fact the zombie apocalypse more precisely fits the shift within capitalism to an abolition of the future and the welcoming of catastrophe as a means to 'wipe the slate clean' and remove fiscal inefficiencies, low productivity, institutional regulation and the social solidarities that stand in the way of its oil-saturated algorithms. Equally, at the scale of personal relations, zombie-like behaviour in the real world has nothing to offer the living: "zombies do what some men imagine doing in the act of sexual penetration and others fear being done to them. They dissolve selfhood through the act of possession" (p.59, Rutherford).

What the zombie mythos reveals is nothing to do with causation in the real world, but something about a productive function that goes on between itself and that world: "the old order is overturning without anything being offered in its place... a nihilistic howl of destructive rage that cannot be assuaged" (p.83, Russell). Did you spot the contradiction? This is a nihilism which does not reduce to nothing, but regenerates itself; for it "cannot be assuaged". This is a mythos *about* a 'fundamental' hunger; an excess energy that, not in every case, but in certain products, or parts of them, turns on itself, reproduces itself in excess, and, as part of doing so, demonstrates the effects of shifts in fictions, images and ideas on real people. There is nothing actual that can be built upon its hypothetical situation; rather it is the combination of its absenting of a future and the putting aside of causality that, together, gives us inspiration and permission to act. That's all.

This book is partly about how to wander to the point where we can abandon the mythos; and it is the very abject nature of the zombie ideal, its de-composing of itself, violent like an earthquake is violent and not how an army is, that can help us. In facing up to the rotting thing that is now preoccupying the thinking where we might have expected to find the best hope – in speculations about the future – we still have a chance at picking our way between the furtive and objectifying intercourse of desperate humans with fantasy objects (utopias and ideal milieus) and the absolute erotic imperatives of charmless ghouls (oil and markets).

In the real world you cannot walk like the erotic zombie. Not yet, for sure. But you can take the forms of its drives and apply them to your own forms. Walk anywhere and everywhere, unfix your eyes from the way ahead or from fine details close to hand and disperse your desiring gaze across the vistas of the most abject and alienated cityscapes. Ignore the romance of the fabulously diverse bodies passing you by and imagine zipless and inconsequential encounters with crowds of bodies in doorways, around forgotten monuments, across the broken tracks of redundant railway stations, over the gritty surfaces of wasteground, inside rusted boilers, deep in the woods; no one will ever see these congresses. There is no gaze in the land of the dead. The zombie can sense to find, but not to appropriate; there is no voyeurism in zombieland and objectification is pointless.

Once you feel yourself immersed in zombie sex, switch back to walking as a survivor. In that switch you will have carried a little of the zombie into the survivor; its "bite... reactivates the entire body as an erogenous zone and takes the focus away from civilized genital contact" (p.202, Clark). More than looking for places of discreet pleasures, you are now about bathing your entire body, coursing with arousal, in the smells, textures, banters, come-ons, swarms and moans of the city.

Ask yourself: is this a subtraction from your humanity or an addition to it?

Later, set about some planning: how might you bathe the city with the kinds of excitements that have been running through your body? This was once the ambition of architects, but is now more the province of comedy-artists like Banksy, with his ironic

*installations barely discernible or discerned from real theme
parks and museums. Or, in fictions, this is the stage for serial
killers like the Lecter of the 'Hannibal' TV series or the villain
of 'True Detective series one' who sculpt their victims into
elaborate public installations. This is not necessarily a bad
thing. It means the field is more open than before.*

*Look at the ornamentation of contemporary retail and civic
spaces; compare it to that on any surviving buildings from one
hundred years ago. There is a transience now, a reliance on
fonts and symbols – the golden arches, the mermaid, the
pecten, the swoosh – rather than materials. Where the
transformation of a city space once required a war or
revolution or a generational re-planning like Haussmann's of
Paris or Le Corbusier's of Chandigarh, today's reliance on
symbols makes the public space of the city both more
vulnerable and more policed; the absurd punctiliousness of
mall security guards is testimony to the rapid affordance of
these spaces. They can no longer rely on doormen controlling
access, but must police ambience and appearance throughout
their democratic spaces.*

*Imagine transforming those elements. Imagine what you could
do with the power of those spaces if you could add your own
symbols; if you could generate atmospheres and impressions
from your own fantasies and associations, release symbols from
your autobiography. Think how you might change the uses of
the ice rinks, the bodies of water in the swimming pools, what
you might drive with the winds that sweep the public squares,
what performances you might enact in the interconnecting lofts
on the top floors of shops on the High Street, or what you might
monitor from the vantage points on the roofs of office blocks.
How you might misuse the pedestrian bridges, the layers of car
parks, the secret mail train tunnels.*

By switching between living dead and survivor, bringing a little of each to the
other, you have taken your zombie walking to a new level; a plane from where
you can shift again later, with the help of a narrative of things, towards what
Dylan Trigg has called a "shared experience [that] conjoins the living and the
nonliving in the same body" (p.33), the opposite of, and the resolution to,

that old gothic conundrum about conflict in a single body.

By now you may be feeling that you have been putting yourself 'out there' enough; even if you have 'only' been imagining yourself doing these walks and making these plans. So that perhaps now is the time to look inwards for a while. Did you think it would be safer there?

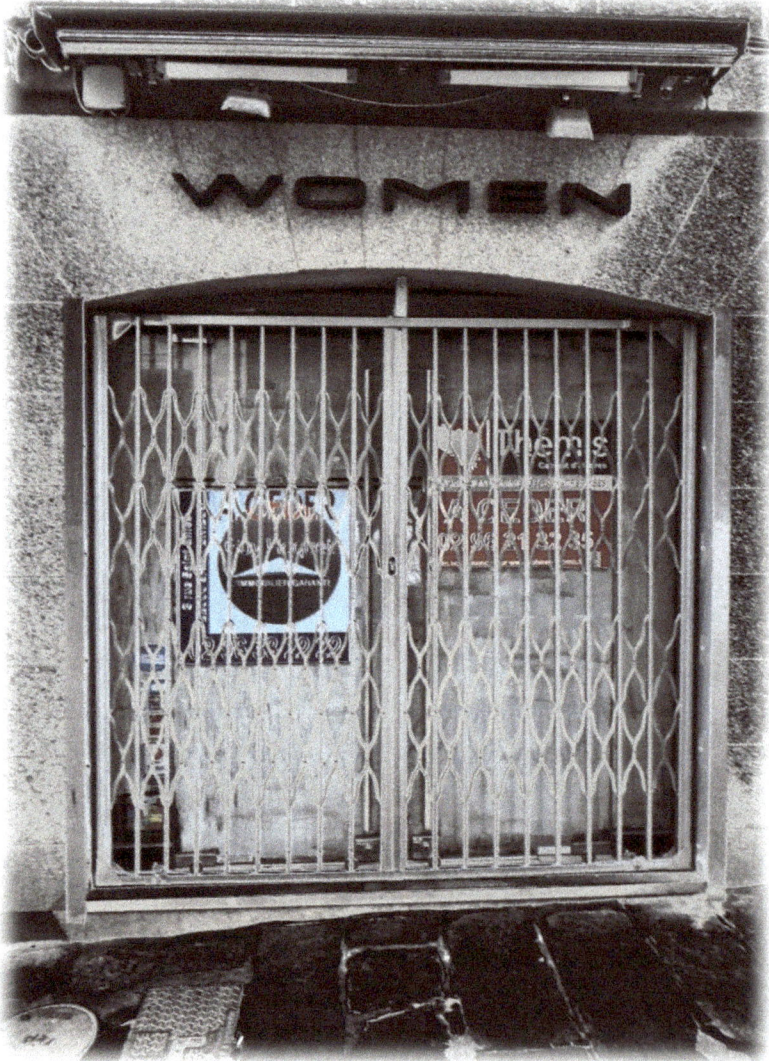

8/ "I've seen The Darkness! It's inside me!"

At the centre of the zombie is nothingness. More subversive than its Marxian representation of the masses is its representation of a space that is different from absence (as there has never been any thing there) or emptiness (as there is no vessel or stage for it). Nothingness is the revolutionary quality that Romero was talking about in 1968. A black hole, a refusal to represent, it destroys everything including destruction, sucking space dry until all that remains is its latent potency and potent latency, its vibrant inanimateness and inanimate vibrancy; it is a darkness smothering all the bases. A world population free from the prison of their souls and facing into a void. A narrative that refuses to replace, to look forward, to give evidence for hope, yet demands something, at the very least despair, to come from nothing.

Nothing can come of nothing, yet nothingness, like a foolish monarch, demands that we speak again.

In an essay for a special issue of the journal 'Studies in Theatre and Performance' on zombie performance (Smith, 2014), I configured the darkness in a zombie brain revealed by Dr Jenner of the Center for Disease Control in an episode of 'The Walking Dead' as a simple absence of 'you'. The empty space left by the death of interiority and subjectivity. The emptiness that some zombies feel a painful need to fill: "more brains!"

But what if this zombie darkness represents less an absence and more a dark distillation? What if zombie darkness is a thickening to intensity of a virtual something, part of a living interiority separate from the brightness of the spectacle, of an "integrity and meaningfulness of human life [that] depend[s] on keeping public and private rigorously distinct... the distinction between things that should be shown and things that should be hidden... That darkness, the place of elemental bodily need and desire... [that] must be hidden from the public realm... because it harbours the things hidden from human eyes and impenetrable to human knowledge" (pp.32-33, Cohen)?

This is not nothing, but nothingness, a "thing is there, present... as a field of anonymity" (p.131, Trigg).

> *Walk with discretion. Walk anonymously and enjoy it. Keep yourself to yourself. Walk privately in public places.*
>
> *Make a walk with friends through retail parks, shopping centres and malls, national chains and designer shops; ignore all their commercial and consumption codes and focus instead on what is economically meaningless (the water in the fountains, the rhythm of the escalators, the patina of the stone cladding). If security guards, shop assistants or managers challenge you, then explain exactly what you are doing. If they ask you to leave do not protest but exit their store as disinterestedly and indifferently as you arrived, and move on to the next retail space. Give no attention to commodities or advertising images and do not participate in any purchasing. There is no need to assume a zombie physicality, simply a corpse indifference to the narrow economic definition of what 'value' is.*

The Kyoto school of philosophers navigate the overlapping terrains of self and world by attention to nothingness; aware that to establish peace across these landscapes it is necessary to find a commonality with the within of the inanimate and to challenge the discrete interiority of the self: "To look at things from the standpoint of the self is always to see things merely as objects, that is, to look at things *without* from a field *within* the self" (p.9, Nishitani). Nothingness collapses these insides and outsides, withins and withouts, replacing binaries with the unity of things: the mystically inclined Kyoto thinkers advocate a not thinking, a refusal to represent and a looking directly at reality, even when it is elusive and invisible, rather than at the finger pointing to it (p.157, Carter). In times of spectacle-domination, this challenge, though metaphysical, to representation is at least prescient. While most materialist radicalisms, given the discrediting of utopia, have lost all sense of what might be to come, by suggesting subtraction, rather than surplus (the usual driver of utopian economies), the Kyoto School at least offer us a private space and a practical tool with and in which to start thinking forward again.

The Kyoto philosophers equate a non-analytical experiencing of reality accessed via nothingness, a phenomenology without phenomena, with a "loving and relying" (157) upon a unity of things that includes and does not distinguish between human and unhuman, animate and inanimate. Attention to the nothingness that is driving this un-knowing experiencing is something we can learn from the living corpse; by imitating its dead-pan, discreet, implacable sincerity ("truly wrapped up in being what [they are]... exhibit[ing] a genuine inner life of [their] own"), its desiring without needing to perform desire and its indifference to spectacle. By nurturing a 'nothingness-that-is-somewhere', a dark within with an affinity to the anonymity of inanimateness, we can have 'to hand' a resistance against the repetition and completionism that transforms each fresh discovery into a thrall, each new possession into being possessed by it. Recognition of the inanimate quality of what is most deep within the hidden part of our selves makes possible a revolutionary pleasure-taking that destroys, by its sincerity and being true to itself, anything it appropriates and anything that tries to appropriate it. Desiring citizens possessed of their own nothingness cannot be recruited; they are radically asocial, they cannot be imposed upon without putting that very fabrication itself in danger of collapse.

They are difficult to live with.

The recognition by a person of the nothingness within them disrupts the 'normal' formations of ideology by interposing a predatory absence into the fabrication of memory from memories.

> *Put a shark in their think tanks. Why? Because if you eventually get round to noticing how much of your memory space is filled up, you will find that the cuckoo is a think tank. (If Lucio Fulci can contrive a fight between a shark and zombie for 'Zombie Flesh Eaters', we can do this.)*

Absence places itself, waving and hollering, where the original event was but is no more, loudly recognising another absence, identifying memories as simulacra and histories as reconstructions from other reconstructions, invoking the lack of anything real at the centre and base of all of them. It shines darkly on order, hope, faith, memory and history, exposing the fragility of all of them, lest we build too heavily upon them and again raise utopias that require torture chambers in their foundations to hold them up and patrol boats off their beaches to separate the corpses from the tourists. What at first appears to be self-destructive – and it will take an effort on your part, if you truly find this nothingness within yourself, not to make life deeply uncomfortable for those around you – is the saving of self through multiplicity, adding darkness to your parts.

> *Walk through the crowds in exact imitation of individual trajectories. Get together with friends to do this in public spaces. Do not follow anyone, simply reproduce the routes, speeds, walking methods, and so on, of individuals crossing the space. Observe people carefully. Then, once they have left the space, imitate their journey. Repeat and repeat and repeat, until by this accumulation of copies, a hyper-camouflage, a living alongside the enemy, a clogging of the foe's advances and supply lines, bottlenecks, jamming and blockages together spasm into the production of a new foe. Move on to the next square.*

By recognising and accepting the darkness within, we can grasp through our actions (loving, relying) that if we are exploiting the fossils then the fossils are also exploiting us; that it is not our 'unnatural' intervention in nature that is bringing us to the edge of an abyss, but that we are always at this edge and that it is nature that is pushing us over. That our ecologically-minded self-lacerations are parts of the hubris that has dragged the Earth into our drama of mutual destruction; and that rather than creating an anthropomorphic narrative of the planet (whether maternal or vengeful) we would do better to embrace its inanimateness.

In terms of the living dead narrative, the zombie is not something to fear, exploit or destroy, but a new kind of developing fossil life (part of its newness is the chemical precipitation of a revenant of a former organism/organisation that persists and cannot disappear), it is something to walk in relation to, sustaining a mutual adventure with, until we find a best way to end the entangled journey and take our places in the darkness. Contemplating, loving and relying on nothingness will not lead us to immortality – we can leave that to sea urchins – but rather to the possibility, like the dead disappearing into darkness beneath the city of 'Les Revenants', of choosing a modest exit. This is the antidote to the violent mythos.

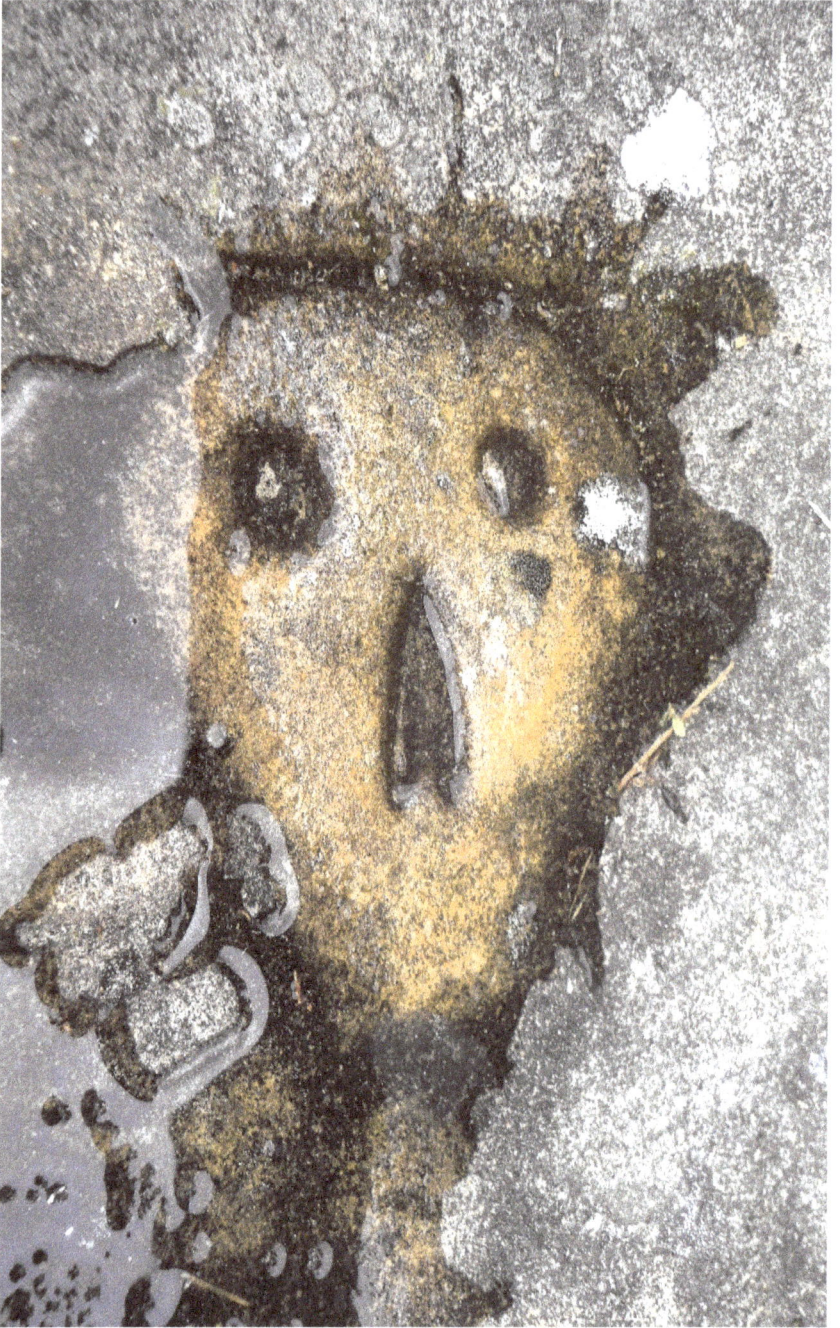

9/ returning

In Robin Campillo's 2004 movie 'Les Revenants' the recently deceased emerge, in an orderly fashion, clean and unruffled, slowly and silently, from (contra Brooks) a city's cemetery. Rather than the resurrection of stiff or flaccid corpses, this is a superficially less messy return of people from attenuated pasts. They exhibit no obvious impulse to predate upon the living. The local state, as public policy, escorts and collectivises the dead, concentrating many of them in an emergency centre where they 'sleep' in a gridded dormitory; they are subjected to what Jack Halberstam calls the 'zombie humanism' of an invasive welfarism and control by care and disempowerment.

The dead seem passive, docile even, doing as they are asked. Some are collected by their families; some seek out less willing families. Their responses are always slightly 'off', but apparently benign. They seem to remember certain things and can participate in what are mostly appropriate conversations. But these are husks of interaction, gestures to meaning rather than holding meaning. Signifiers float free of signifieds, making explicit the actual process of memory as a remembering only of memories. They suffer from "a lack of synchronisation with reality".

Like the conventional zombie "they tend to wander". At night, the dead drift off from the emergency centre and from their old homes. These nocturnal journeys seem to be random, or returns, by habit, to familiar places; however, a relative who follows one of the dead discovers that they are holding meetings. They are planning something.

> *You can take this kind of wandering as a model: 'on the surface'*
> *it is a meaningless jumble of turnings and chance connections,*
> *an enigmatic winding through time and space, but from*
> *within, from the perspective of the wanderers, it is a weaving of*
> *coherent and consistent journeying, a knot: "from the outside...*
> *a mess of intersecting bits, like a devil's street map. But*
> *conceived intrinsically, experienced, as it were, it has a*

consistency, despite its twists and turns. It is the 'same' rope, no matter how its angle varies" (p.17, Wark).

Walk through the city, making as many knots and twists in your route as you can, while maintaining a single objective or drive to your journey.

That continuity through a single trajectory of change, consistent between the outside and the inside, in a knot-like 'situational dérive' is a pilgrimage and an intervention, changing the entangled self and terrain simultaneously. This has the same dynamics as the 'geographical aesthetics' proposed by Harriet Hawkins and Elizabeth Straughan: "marked by a sense of entanglement... of humans and non-humans... potential to rework that wrenching duality, replacing it instead with the eternal twists and turns of the Möbius strip" (pp.285-6).

If there are friends or acquaintances who are also using this book, arrange to zombie walk simultaneously and separately but in the same district, allowing the meander to bring you together in 'chance' meetings. Share the consistencies of your rope, or strip, and knot them with those of your fellow walkers. Together, plan something.

Well-meaning attempts at integration of the dead of 'Les Revenants' founder. They are incapable of innovation, they can only do repetition; white collar dead are demoted to blue collar work.

Walk, and as you do, invent an action – say, walk five steps, stop and look up and then walk on – repeat this slavishly.

At night increasing numbers of the deceased gather in crowds quietly chanting directions. Eventually, they make their move, sabotaging the city, turning terrorist, setting off explosions and making a break across the city park for nothingness. In their exodus some of the dead are gassed by the military, but many of them make it to tunnels under the city. Into which, and within which, they disappear, a reversal of a zombie re-birth. They are darkness returning to darkness, nothingness that rightfully returns to nothingness; "our infantile desire for immortality... gone deep into the unconscious" (p.190, Asma). A death that is wholly separate from living.

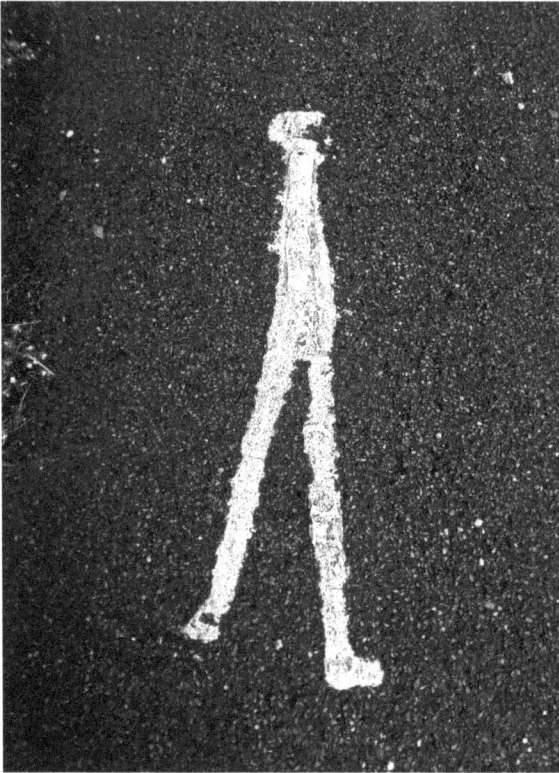

A woman who only reluctantly took back her dead husband now follows him to the darkness beneath the city. The tunnels do not lead to hell, nor unholy gatherings of the undead; instead, they lead to the silence and darkness of the grave. She is left alone.

Sometimes translated as 'The Returned' or 'They Come Back', 'Les Revenants' might be better translated as 'They Go Back' or 'The Leavers', for it is the departure and separation of the dead from the living, and the respect for a darkness beneath, between and within, that this film is all about.

> *Walk until you find the darkness, the nothingness, beneath and within your city.*

> *Walk in search of those places in your city – they may be rare and difficult to find (blood transfusion services, second-hand book shops, perhaps) – where a relation to things gives hope of choosing a good way for us all to end.*

10/ a taxonomy of morbid cities

Unlike war, earthquake, invasion or most other apocalypses, the zombie catastrophe leaves the built environment pretty much as it is. Clumsy resistance sets a few fires, there's some looting, but structurally things stay mostly as they are. It is space that is transformed. Places begin to wizen and become fusty by disuse and malfunction rather than destruction, the city of the living dead is dried and emptied rather than razed. Other representations of disaster are more prurient in their treatment of architecture; zombie movies are reserved and respectful of the surfaces and structure of place, but radical when it comes to "the destruction of hegemonic and ideological spatial codifications (public/private, etc.)... streets are for moving cars, hospitals are for helping the ill, etc." (pp.286 & 294, May).

> *It takes only a little imagination to see the living dead city lying just beneath or beyond the surface of yours. It is a palimpsest that history has not yet got round to laying down or etching out. Your city can be explored from just to the side of itself, from a vantage point that is neither above nor wholly immersed, but just a little unfamiliar.*
>
> *Choose a space. Re-designate its function. Use it accordingly. Use it prefiguratively. A post office as an art gallery. A pub as a council chamber. A waste bin as a confessional.*
>
> *This is also a shift in your zombie walking, moving through and beyond your own feelings, associations and experiences to a focus on and into the spaces themselves. This is not a standing back or being distanced and objective, but a handing over to the spaces by being more deeply in them.*
>
> *Once you have adopted more of the qualities of the driven dead you will find yourself crossing more boundaries; making*

> *sudden shifts between residential and industrial, large plots*
> *and disenfranchised projects/estates, sliding along the sharp*
> *edges between suburbia and the fields.*

Jeff May describes the emergence in the living dead mythos of a new kind of space: "the city's main operating functions are destroyed and everyday actions are drastically altered... the soft spaces of the city are writ clean, reduced to blank space... new functions can be chosen for rigid spaces such as military bases, hospitals, office buildings" (p.290). This sudden unveiling of the potency and metamorphosing qualities of city space is similar to an urban wanderer arriving in what Francisco Careri has described as 'voids': "an enormous quantity of empty spaces that form the background against which the city defines itself... different from those open spaces traditionally thought of as public spaces – squares, boulevards, gardens, parks... an enormous portion of undeveloped territory... the last place in the city where we can feel we are beyond surveillance and control... a public space with a nomadic character" (pp.181 & 184).

> *Find a field empty of people, livestock and crops, walk into it;*
> *make sure that you have a view over an expanse of ground. Feel*
> *the security given by your sweeping gaze, and then how that*
> *viewpoint exposes you to another gaze, though there is no one*
> *to see you. This gaze without a gazer (rather like dread's*
> *anxiety without a threat) is the 'malevolent gaze', it is what*
> *obliges us and what we adapt ourselves to even when*
> *unobserved, the keeper of our obligation to expectations of us*
> *that are not our own, it is whatever we feel we have to 'live up*
> *to' and dare not exceed. It is what we fear will punish us if we*
> *hide in darkness. The existential threat of disappearance if we*
> *do not perform.*
>
> *Here in the 'freedom' of the open field feel the eyes upon you*
> *and resolve to throw them off.*

It is not only in redundant or abandoned spaces that a 'blankness' reveals itself. In the opening scenes of 'Land of the Dead', a small town has been "fruitfully taken up on its potential by the resident zombies" (May, 295); these zombies perform a deconstructed repetition, like a literary lettrism or musical minimalism of past behaviours. The mishandling and tooting on wind instruments in the town's gazebo are like a postmodern music-making in which the materiality of the instruments is as important as their sound productions, and tunes are broken down into single notes.

This is a process of re-personification via living death; 'blankness' in body overlain on 'blankness' in space. These emptinesses do not just suck in meat, but pop up new elements; a creativity that borrows from the post-human without conceding its subjectivity. Through Johnny, Bub, Number 9, and so on, it is a reconstituting of a new subject from the imagined ruins of a "process of self-preservation... based on the bourgeois division of labour... of individuals, who must mold themselves to the technical apparatus body and soul" (p.23, Horkeimer & Adorno). This is the vital secret that is buried beneath the mounds of the mythos's corpses and in the ruins of the 'decontaminated' Center for Disease Control lab in 'The Walking Dead': the 'blankness' of the living dead is not mindless, but the emerging of a new kind of mind. And, complementarily, of how "horror awakens thought shockingly to its intimate and inescapable connectedness to flesh" (p.5, Morgan).

What follows is a limited taxonomy of zombie 'blank spaces where you might attempt similar re-personifications. These are generic locations that are not 'just there', but emerge from suspended potential due to the "transfer of bodily ambiguity to city space" (p.297, May). You are not simply visiting these places; you are re-making them, performing them as you perform yourself, into spaces that can become new.

I have often observed well-intentioned and competently delivered community-targeted public art initiatives that come and go, brighten a space for a while, but do not change it. No great harm in that. I have seen other, odder performances – a mis-guided tour into a derelict communal drying area, an allusive and gentle autobiographical performance (to which the police were called) among the roadside bramble-hidden stones of an old gateway, a promenade cabaret climaxing in a boxing match – where the disruptive and the 'to-the-side' quality of the interventions, to some extent actually *at odds* with the community of these places, has provoked a changing of their sites: the tidying of the drying space and the recommencement of hanging washing there, the clearing of the brambles and the preservation of the gateway's stones, the re-opening for community use of a neo-classical temple. In all these cases I am fairly certain that the residents and officials responsible for the changes would deny any agency to the performances; and that is their power. They work at an oblique angle, not engaging directly with perceived 'needs' nor insisting upon any community agenda, but allusively, suggestively, in the nudging and irritating besideness of performance. The collective, accidentally co-operative and peaceful zombie actions described above, by a similar 'blankness' and besideness, work similarly upon such spaces; drawing attention not to themselves, but to the incongruities and space-producing dynamics between bodies and places.

Voids...

...partly by its near-paranoid approach and partly by its facility for finding odd and less visited places, zombie walking, in common with 'drifting' and a mythogeographical sensitivity, will bring you to the city's voids, big and small. These are places where urban development, no matter how planned, runs out of energy, or forgets, or mis-measures, or shifts suddenly without preparation, or just flees. (Romero invented a void for 'Dawn', setting his mall in an apparent wasteland; when in fact its actual location is crowdedly suburban.) These are abandoned zones, or overlooked margins; vast swathes of Detroit or parts of the post-industrial English North and Midlands, or simply a verge or ornamental border that is no longer maintained. While speculation on housing has forced up land prices in the more comfortable parts of England, bringing back into the economy even tiny pieces of waste ground, the accompanying winnowing of public spending has seen new voids opening up in previously well-ordered parks and playgrounds. In some cases, the paving of public squares has subsided or risen out of the horizontal plane and pedestrians skirt around the edges. The smoothness of public space, the facilitating of a mindless passage through the grounds of what once were politics, the *agora*, is unevenly wrinkled now; the phantoms on the flat screens are disturbed. These small details of disruption are presentiments of the city to come, the trip hazards that will put a torque on relentless progress.

There are temporary voids too. Often I have walked, on a weekday afternoon, through ghost towns: deserted suburban streets, empty playgrounds, silent greens. (A word of caution is required, however. These affordant 'non-places' of the zombie outbreak do sound suspiciously like colonial fantasies of an 'empty land'; nothing has not been bitten.) As much as in any pen or prison, in the privileged suburb you will feel the savage compartmentalisation in affluent lives (the poor have no such luxuries), the demarcations that deregulation brings between time and space. After wandering one such commuter village, undisturbed, for a couple of hours I returned to its small railway platform; joined by two freemasons, dark suits and black briefcases, one learning his ritual from a small red book; anachronisms to sustain the space of modern ordinariness.

Surburbia...

...empty streets – even the most faceless – are alive with possibility once you are zombie walking. At any moment they will not, or are most unlikely to, explode into the mayhem of that early scene from the remake of 'Dawn' when nurse Ana escapes by car from her re-animated partner. Yet the scene that she swerves and accelerates through is implicit in every suburban silence and stasis. It is the consumption-fuelled, viral, catastrophic 'free' and autonomous market got up on its feet and running about, instinctive, grabbing, biting, chasing and abruptly changing its direction under the tyranny of endless choices that the suburb brings to a standstill. The suburb freezes the ecstatic city in the order of its clipped hedgerows and shaved lawns, yet it can never wholly deny its urban, dromological tempo which escapes in barks, in the rapid whirring of lawnmower blades and the hasty departures of adulterers' cars. These are the antechambers of the free-market extreme, the preserved spoils of choice without concern for consequences; in zombie movies such vehicles quickly become traps. Few move for long; 'Big Daddy' is the universal gas station attendant in zombieland and the pump at his station is dry. It is, without intention, a 'greener' place.

The parallel city...

...zombie walking will give you access to a 'parallel city'. You will discover that alongside the everyday routes and paths there are other ways of moving about, tracks kept worn by animals or those hermit humans that you very rarely see, service roads, gaps between one development and another and unvisited grounds where the long and unbroken grass tells you that you are the first human there for some time.

> Seek out the parallel city. Follow animal tracks. Walk only in back alleys and sunken lanes. On major thoroughfares walk off sideways looking for hidden routes running parallel to the official ones. Map the meshwork of your shadow city and share.

Walking aimlessly around a small rural town I began to feel out older routes among the mini-suburbs, across the centres of large roundabouts, down the less travelled of green lanes, drovers routes and sunken ways, ancient routes preserved or missed by planners and ignored by residents, wondering idly whether the dead would take the green hilltop routes, or follow the streams in the now developed valleys.

Given the complex interconnectedness of the city's technical needs and the disconnection of its social behaviours, there is necessarily some fraying of physical space; you can walk these trailing threads. Your walking can thus become an ambiguous parody of the alienations and ironies of the city; an exaggeration of its disconnectedness and a refusal of it.

> Sitting on a railway station platform. All these people, all these fabrications, all these processes, hung on a meshwork of relations. Change those relations and they disappear. I watch the other passengers, trains come and go, passengers board, red light to green light, and then, in my head, it all shuts down and from the thin veil of the day I can feel the dust blown ankle deep

in the corners of the Starbucks cafe, the shadows falling on rusty tracks, crows on the stairs, the dull dark grey of the screens. It doesn't look that different, but what is novel is the dramatic entrance of nothing. This is the city Cillian Murphy's Jim glimpses for a few minutes at the start of '28 Days Later'. Find a seat in the city. Watch a busy space. In your head, subtract the people. What relations can you read in what is left?

You will also find in this 'parallel city' a terrain of wonders; it is a very different sensation when you arrive by accident and without warning at some relic of the past poking up through a modern housing estate, or if the ruins of a shopping centre open up to a wide-sweeping vista, than if you arrive by design clutching a guidebook and already knowing what you are going to see, pre-experiencing every place through its images.

Twin pillars...

...you may see these in various manifestations. Where a road sign has been knocked off its poles. Where two bollards serve to block a path against larger vehicles. In freemasonry these are the two pillars of the temple, resilience on the one side and a first grounding on the other. In your apocalyptic landscape you might like to think of them as an invitation to pass between false alternatives described by Susan Sontag as "two equally fearful, but seemingly opposed, destinies: unremitting banality and inconceivable terror" (p.224, Sontag, 2009), and into their conceivable hybrid: banal terror open to remittance.

Wounded city...

...you will see where the city spills its guts. Sometimes literally; I am still shocked at finding a large and unexplained pool of blood on a suburban street in a 'genteel' Swiss town. More likely the guts will be allusive ones: huge tubes like intestines, drainage pipes and culverted rivers, ventilation shafts and crawlspaces full of spaghetti wires. Those of you who understand how to safely place-hack will climb inside the body of the city, flow with its flow, immersed in its harsh viscera; a body inside a body. In there, you might sense the twitching of the restless iron inside your own flesh and bone: "the interior third of terrestrial mass, semifluid metallic ocean, megamolecule and pressure-cooker beyond imagination... plutonic science slides continuously into schizophrenic delirium" (pp.498-499, Land).

As well as the churchyards and crematoria, you might pay particular attention to other forms of waste disposal and treatment; or even attend more closely to what it is that is served as food in the town's eateries.

Demand a raw freshness. You might look more closely at the contents of bins and skips and eye suspiciously the activities of cleaners and disposal workers.

The whole modern zombie mythos begins in a graveyard with a brother and sister unable to reconcile themselves to a satisfactory relationship with the dead, arguing about a chore for their mother, putting flowers on a grave. Even the characters of the 'Resident Evil' franchise, with its futuristic bio-tech catastrophe, manage to find their way to an infected cemetery. The Neapolitan philosopher Vico, in the imaginary prehistory of his *The New Science* (1725), describes the marking of graves as one of the first signs of a civil society emerging in bright clearings from the loneliness and brutality of dark forests where the dead lay where they fell. How long will it be before escalating prices of building land inspire venture capitalists to broach this marker of 'civilisation', stack the carved stones and dispatch the bones to publicly funded ossuaries and begin to dig foundations? Is it those Gnostic cadavers, empty as their coffins, popping up in the uncompleted swimming pool in 'Poltergeist' (1982), puppets jiggled by the invisible hand of a regulated market, that are holding them back? Or is it the uneasy thought that "a hierarchy based on a metric of 'civilisation'" (p.24, Saunders), the justification for everything from the colonisation of 'empty' lands to the 'wars on terror' and 'wars against the subjugation of women and the destruction of monuments', might slip if we began to inhabit in large numbers an anti-'civilisation' of remade loneliness in dark social forests?... if we swarmed in ones, Poe-esque 'men (sic) of the crowd', manic as Lovecraft, staring vacantly and unmoved at commodities as if they were so many headstones, buying nothing and buying into nothing, stalking "without apparent object", and luring spectators "wearied unto death" into a performance of the city's 'heart' which cannot be consumed as spectacle (from Edgar Allan Poe, 'The Man of the Crowd')?

Spend time in graveyards; they are underestimated architectural and textual lexicons, irony clusters, paused spaces for the contemplation of the changing materials of real lives, no less current for having passed. Sit still and listen to what sings there.

Haunted spaces...

...even in the most modern of estates there is some revenant returning. Sometimes these are artful interventions; witty restorations that then outwit their renovators. Sometimes they are the results of irreconcilable obstacles; the 'listing' of a building or a space of special scientific or historical interest. Sometimes they are opportunistic; the planners using an old village pond (barely recognisable now as such) as a balancing pool for the drainage of a new estate (these giant constructions in the landscape can never be wholly unmindful of the local ecology). Or the relics of a simple forgetfulness. The remnant of a cut and laid hedge in a children's playground slowly growing into a line of trees. Such revenants make themselves known, though they are ignored by residents anaesthetised by their familiarity and redundancy; when you get there you will feel the peculiar tug of their hunger. For these are the ravenous things of the city. Shorn of their historic character they are desperate for some agent or actor to perform them again. You will feel them reach out to you like hordes not wholly restrained by wire fences. Don't stay too long in their presence. Those that do stay become possessed; experts in animated minutiae or micro-localists. Historiography (not what happened, but the obsessive drive to repeat it) when not wed to anticipation, when not understood as materials to come (see DeSilvey *et al*) is the most morbid spectacle of all, out-doing even Comrade Trotsky's silent picture shows.

Not only 'edgelands'...

...evacuated spaces have become increasingly attractive to site-based performance makers and other space artists. Since Marion Shoard introduced the 'edgelands' neologism and her description of an indeterminate, unmaintained and thinly populated space on the edges of cities as "the only theatre in which the real desires of real people can be expressed" (p.140, Shoard), the impulse among some artists and performance makers to work in cities and yet away from people has found a new legitimisation. At the third and final Performing Place Symposium (Chichester, UK, 2015), writer and academic Katie Beswick made a powerful attack on this tendency which implies that the central public and social places that are most important to city dwellers, particularly working class ones, for the purposes of arts and performances at least, are 'off the map'.

So, make people your destination. Invent scenarios where you enact the same improvisations with strangers as you might in apocalyptic conditions; you may be surprised how many people are already living their own private infections and apocalypses.

Even in the 'voids' it is the potential for re-use by the living, not their 'emptiness', that is important.

Abandoned theme parks...

...and now I will contradict myself. Hayao Miyazaki got it right in 'Spirited Away': these are worlds. There is something especially resonant about abandoned leisure parks and their miniature equivalents. No matter how banal or limited they have been, abject model railways, abandoned funfairs still on their lorries and cobwebbed window displays were all once attempts to create a utopia from play. They are inebriated hiccups that ran out of breath. Whether by nostalgia or futurism, comic absurdity (Blobbyland!) or archaeological fantasy, these places are reminders of just how deathly utopia can be when made for real. You will find them at the climaxes of 'Nightmare City' and 'Zombieland', and perhaps at their most beautiful in the landscape of abandoned concrete 'prehistoric monsters', redundancy on top of extinction, on the outskirts of Berlin in Bruce LaBruce's 'Otto: or Up With Dead People!' (2008)

Visit derelict or poorly maintained model villages, theme parks and museums. These spectral remains of literal idealism, of being driven by ideas more than by anything else, are to be greedily valued among all the repetitive honeytraps of commodity obsession. Hold your séances there. Go hunting intellectual ghosts. In these tombs of hope you will find the shade of an older hopefulness; in the dim outlines of temples, arts of memory and symbolic landscapes. Write a manifesto there.

Whatever ideas are conjured from these sites, never let them take command. Strangely, for a game of cannibals, it is from ideas like these that you are most in danger; they will quickly gobble you up into abstruse towers of practical application and speculative planning. (For which you need quite different ideas from the ones here.) Keep telling yourself, whenever you feel the impulse to turn any of this into a constructed place, that shopping malls were first proposed by a socialist planner to promote communitarian spaces and the contemporary city of raised and culverted motorised flows is an adaptation of the ambulatory city, New Babylon, proposed by situationist architect Constant Nieuwenhuys. The value of ideas to you is in their severance from immediate realisation.

If you feel the pull of application... walk away.

Traps...

...the bunkers and pill boxes of earlier wars; fought and unfought. Prisons, army bases, churches. Laboratories. Banks. Gated communities. And those poisonous hybrids and improvisations enacted in 'Zombie 108' (2012) and 'Wyrmwood' (2014) (see below in 'Swarm Politics'). They may also come in the form of pens; small fenced enclosures like those underground in 'Day of the Dead' or in 'The Dead Next Door' (1989).

These cages appear where the living have enough control and motivation to try to police the dead; restraining, goading, torturing and experimenting. The pens, though, can work both ways; as assembly points for the monsters. There is a recognisable moment in the mythos when the fences all give way and the shambling horde is released as an invigorated collective, overwhelming the humans by the wave-like force of numbers.

> *As a tactic at a political demonstration or procession, try policing yourselves into tight groups that then break out, as if on the collapses of a fence or a line of cops, spilling in one direction. Then form up again until you break free once more. Practise this pulsing of surging energy. Rather than the uniform pace of a plodding march.*

Where you come across these pens you may note that what has been restrained is not the living dead, but the living; these pens often seal off former public spaces or formerly accessible 'informal' spaces where private or state ownership had not previously been a bar to entry. Under the auspices of safety or protection of property the body of the city is increasingly segregated; the stitching between the different parts undone like a body in a French new-extremity movie like 'In My Skin' or 'Thanatomorphose'.

Vistas...

...in the aftermath of the destruction of the twin towers in New York on September 11th 2001, it was repeatedly remarked that, despite the unprecedented nature of the attacks, there was something eerily familiar about them, "accustomed as we are to seeing New York blasted by aliens ('Independence Day') and flattened by tidal waves ('Armageddon')" (p.114, Dave Kerr, quoted in Dixon). Given the familiarity of the zombie mythos (it is rare for me to be asked by anyone what I exactly mean by it) have we now reached a similar level of cultural accommodation to the prospects of threatening and deserted spaces driving our communal or social exchanges indoors and curtailing our means to individual movement.

Abandoned cars, in artfully arranged confusion, are a signature for the beginning of a movie apocalypse. This image forefronts itself in the low budget 'Autumn' (2009) when the viewer can clearly see open road stretching far beyond the few ruined motors amassed in the foreground.

> *Construct a similar irony for yourself, when you come upon an abandoned motor, tires deflated, or the remnants of a breakdown or accident yet to be cleared away. Use these exceptions to colour the vista before you with the prospect of fuel shortages, the consequences of bad climate politics or algorithm driven economic breakdown; now navigate these spaces without the benefit of civil society and without mechanical or electronic devices. Walk the space as blank; signs no longer meaningful, human activity nailed to its own survival interests and to be avoided. Walk the future of loneliness, walk the hopeless irony that the malfunction and redundancy of those instruments we tend to blame most for self-centredness – cars, computers, smartphones – will not push us back towards each other, but further away.*
>
> *Walk beyond these common senses and beyond 'just the way things are' to a space without both; start to run a phantasmagoria across your mind to disrupt this horrifying vista, this landscape without figures: it may include a tail with an eye in the end, an association of pirates recruited among your acquaintances, guerrilla seed-bombing of official spaces, networks of walkways to link all the rooftops in your city, infiltration of governments by poets; it may include the worship of the angels in Wim Wenders' movie 'Wings of Desire', organised stalking of dandelion seeds and the hunting of winds, the collective welcoming of refugees, chalking temple groundplans onto suburban sidewalks, replacement of metro trains by giant worms, the election of fossils and mountains to high office, the casting of double-agents in soap operas and holding prayer meetings for pets: all of this is happening right now. In you. In the city of you. Once you've finished this book, you might want to forget about zombies and follow some of these other narratives.*

The topographical situation in the Tom Savini remake of 'Night' is succinctly characterised by a character, Ben, as "hell on earth... pure hell on earth". The landscapes in US-based living dead movies since 1968 are created by slipping one space across another. In the 1920s and 1930s the Caribbean settings for exotic zombie films were unreal, but fixed. In his 'Night', George Romero moved an American vision of Vietnam and Cambodia and laid it over rural Pennsylvania. Unfamiliar tactics, combatants who seemed to appear out of nowhere, weird motivations such as collectivity and self-sacrifice; these constitute the uncanny of the post-1968 zombie movie. It brings war onto US territory.

Subsequent films, with their stumbling monsters, look like the aftermath of air strikes somewhere far from their likely location. The horror is that 'these things don't happen here'. And the dawning realisation that they either do (lynchings) or they might (uprisings) or they have: in 1985, the same year as Dan O'Bannon released his 'Return of the Living Dead', depicting a limited nuclear strike called from the luxury of a gated mansion against a US town by its own military, Pennsylvania State Police bombed the West Philadelphia commune of a small, mostly African American group called MOVE. The commune and 65 neighbouring houses were destroyed. Eleven people, including five children, died. In Europe the wave of living dead movies that traipsed after 'Dawn' regularly dragged a mis-remembered colonial territory into Europe: the 'Guerreros de Oriente' of the Blind Dead series, "brought back from their last crusade Eastern necromantic secrets of life and death" (p.74, Pulliam).

In the 21st century the spread of zombie movies to a wider range of national cinema industries has produced a new dynamics of place, often very different to the US model; in 2011's Cuban 'Juan of the Dead'/'Juan de los Muertos' the kinds of ruination and malfunction that occur after the apocalypse (malfunctioning lifts, decaying buildings, cars breaking down) are everyday conditions prior to it. The movie's most striking display of soulless collectivism is a street meeting of a neighbourhood Committee for the Defence of the Revolution; when the authorities call for a demonstration against the 'dissidents' it is, of course, the perfect forum for infection. The ruling joke of 'Juan', which makes it a comic-horror, but not a horrific comedy, is that much that is everyday in Cuba continues as before despite the apocalypse. The most significant territorial displacement within the film is the ever-present possibility of crossing the water to Miami – even the living dead (viewed by Juan, his head in the ocean) are making that journey. The film ends with Juan's refusal to leave as he waves off his daughter and his friends. Turning to face the racing horde, his hope is not in change ("you're like this country – things happen to you, but you never change") but in survival: "I'm a survivor. I survived Mariel, I survived the special period, and that thing that came after". For all his roguish charm, Juan is the horror: the thing that repeats the pain of the past, the thing that just goes on and on and on.

Post-9/11, the remake of 'Dawn' by Zack Snyder makes an explicit claim about the nature of the new and alien territory that has come to the US: Islam. After initial hectic scenes of attack, infection and reanimation, the credits sequence begins with a shot of a large congregation of Muslims at prayer. It interleaves mayhem in an infected US with real footage of street battles in the Middle East; finally, an Arab zombie sweeps past a woman in a niqab to attack a US journalist. The message is very clear; the alien terrain that has now arrived is an intellectual, cultural, political and spiritual one. Just as the US was fighting a war against an idea (its 'war on terror') so an idea was now fighting a war on the movie version of the US.

It is remarkable how explicit this image from Zack Snyder's movie is.

Footage of armed militants can blur, Christian armies in Africa and nationalist militias in the Ukraine can appear similar in terms of kit and behaviour. But this image of Muslims at prayer is presented as iconic of a culture, making none of the distinctions that Muslims themselves might make (Shias from Sunnis, for example). It offers the whole-culture-of-Islam as The Monster; the simultaneous bowing of the worshippers framed not as the action of a group of individuals but as the movement of a single roaring organism.

Romero's 'Land' appeared the year after Snyder's 'Dawn'; remarkably for an otherwise intelligent and insightful critic of the zombie mythos, Kevin J. Wetmore follows Snyder's associations and interprets the intelligent zombies of 'Land' as "terrorists... they look like us, but they are out to change and overthrow our society" (p.210). These are particularly odd kinds of terrorist; at the end of the movie, led by Big Daddy and Number 9, they abandon their predations in favour of a self-directed dérive. In Wetmore's zombie universe the "they're us, we're them" is superficial; they just *look* like us, but essentially they are not, they are not "us", they are not "US", and "we" are not like them because "we" do not want to change, "we" only want to survive. On the mutable terrain of the zombie movie, Cuba and the US have reanimated as reactionary twins.

(You can find supplementary taxonomies of zombie space in my articles 'Performative walking in zombie towns' [2014] and 'A taxonomy of 'zombie space' for walking in monstrous cities' [submitted].)

11/ la horde

There is a scene early on in the second of the 'Resident Evil' franchise movies, 'Apocalypse' (2004) where police and military are stationed at the city limits holding back refugees who are fleeing an outbreak of zombie infection that has escaped the underground laboratories beneath Raccoon City, the company town of the Umbrella Corporation. Predictably, the trapped refugees are swiftly converted into a horde of animated, hungry and infectious corpses. The visual message is very clear: refugees = monstrous horde. An infantryman's account of The Zombie War makes the same point differently: "the refugees streaming down the freeway were leading the dead right to us" (p.93, Brooks).

In the French movie, 'La Horde' (2009), there is very little in the way of visual representation of the crowds of living dead that have laid siege to the run down multi-storey blocks of a working class Parisian housing estate. This disparity is more evident than real, however; for what the characters of 'La Horde' struggle with is less an external threat of physical predation and far more the harrowing effects of an internalised post-colonialism running amok inside one of Le Corbusier's anti-revolutionary 'vertical streets'. The semi-derelict block serves as a cabinet of colonial curiosities, the unpromising chamber for a desperate debate between a rogue unit of cops out for revenge and their targets, a partly African gang who have turned the tables on the cops and taken them prisoner; only for the zombie apocalypse to give all the tables an extra tweak.

The criminal gang members, with their roots in France's former colonies, and the predominantly white police squad weave their way through the labyrinthine high rise and around each other's perceptions, prejudices and histories. This shared apocalyptic predicament is insufficient to banish their differences; rather it opens up just how deep, resilient and intimate those differences are. There is none of the 'putting aside' in order to perform unity in the face of the monstrous. Instead, it is their very disunity which opens up the monstrous, 'lifting the veil' on "those things which cannot be included in the real of the openly visible without rupturing the very oppositions that make the whole enterprise move forward" (pp.5 & 8, Williams).

At the centre of what elsewhere (Smith, submitted) I have, in proposing taxonomies of zombie spaces, called a *contested labyrinth*, 'La Horde's' unstable hybrid of cop/criminal gang finds a symbolic monster: a lonely, hermit-like, axe-dragging (a shot which in both its over-worked familiarity and its focus on 'the thing' rather than the man screams "ideological relic!") veteran of France's imperialist military adventures in Vietnam. Imprisoned in his own delusions, he is still 'at war', defending the appropriations and prejudices that have served him so badly. The veteran bitterly personifies the repetitions and scleroses of a morbid but still virulent past. In contrast to the unhinged and yet unchanging predatory nostalgia of this monster, the members of the cop/criminal gang interrogate their pasts as they go, 'discussing' (usually in the form of hurled abuse) neo-colonial politics in Africa and their motives for crime, violence and revenge, as they battle their way down to the ground floor of the high-rise.

These unlikely collaborators seem to be struggling towards some semblance of shared rhetorical and ideological ground level that lies beyond the enclosed space of the tower block. But the cliché is not consummated. The movie's ending is unreservedly bleak, yet also strangely uplifting for being so direct and steadfast in its gaze upon the probabilities. The last two survivors break free from the deadly labyrinth, one from either side of the post-colonial divide. The prospect of a deep reconciliation and solidarity on the 'level playing field' of species-species is ended abruptly by the last surviving cop as she executes the last surviving gangster. This murder completes the revenge mission which begins the film and which the viewer has long forgotten; a sharp and shocking reminder that the monstrous revenant lives on, not just in the dirty and lonely flat of a deluded old mind, but in the assumptions and emotions of a modern, young Parisian white woman. Then something even more interesting happens; the cop's silencing of the debate around the post-colonial question is revealed as suicidal. No sooner has the sound of the gunshot begun to die away among the blocks of the housing estate than its echoes are overwhelmed by the excited sounds of the ravenous horde, pinpointing the conflict for the first time. We do not see the crowd; for they are an idea of what is to come. The modern European no longer has the option of blanking out a past rushing to meet them; the participation of West

European governments in those various 'wars on terror' that have annihilated a number of Arab economies and left the peoples of secular dictatorships to the tender mercies of armed theocrats has made mass immigration inevitable.

The lesson, if there could be such a thing, of 'Resident Evil: Apocalypse' is that 'holding the horde at the wall' is an infection in itself, generating speculative economies of violence based on the resulting variables on different sides of a barrier; binaries that living/dead begins to breaks down in a fiction, but never quite can. The problem of this fiction, hobbled by ideology, is exemplified in Max Brooks and Ibraim Roberson's comic book 'Recorded Attacks' (2009). Zombie outbreaks across 62,000 years are described in ways that either substitute themselves for, or make metaphorical, historical episodes of resistance to slavery, colonial rule and imperialist expansion. What these anti-racist, anti-colonial narratives leave unaccounted for, however, is their own viewpoint; the reports are almost all recorded by those from the colonising West (Sir Francis Drake, "a British dig", and so on) and are of events that happen almost exclusively among the enslaved, excluded or colonised, "inextricably linking non-Western space with monstrosity... us[ing] the hoary trope of cannibalism, a 'linchpin' of the Othering process in the 'European imagination'" (p.24, Saunders). No better than Fulci, then. No surprise either that this particular corpse rises again at the end of the movie adaptation of Brooks' 'World War Z' when a young black woman is zombified and trapped in a glass cell for 'study'; despite the modern trappings of a WHO laboratory the context is uncannily and uncomfortably similar to an ethnographic exhibit at a 19th-century World's Fair (when I saw this movie in the cinema, white audience members giggled derisively at this character); it is a return to that fixing of 'other' that the Romero canon, while itself an appropriation ("dispel[ling] the dark fury of the slave and, in turning the iconography inside out, mak[ing] the zombie's insatiable hunger figure the white consumer instead" [p.97, Lauro & Embry]), has been mostly about dispersing.

The zombie walk or flash mob may, in general, be "an ironic kind of resistance against mainstream culture and values" (p.193, do Vale). It has also been deployed at various kinds of public protest – in support of gay marriage ("IT'S NOT NECROPHILIA IF WE'RE BOTH DEAD"), against library, university and school cuts, disrupting retailing as part of anarchist games (pp.288-289, Lauro), and so on. But its full militant force may only emerge when those who are still enslaved by new imperialisms, racist segregations or sexist subjugations, those who have in uprising shouted "We have no mother, no child; what is death?", can re-appropriate their abjection and give birth to themselves as something new. I won't pretend to know what that might be like.

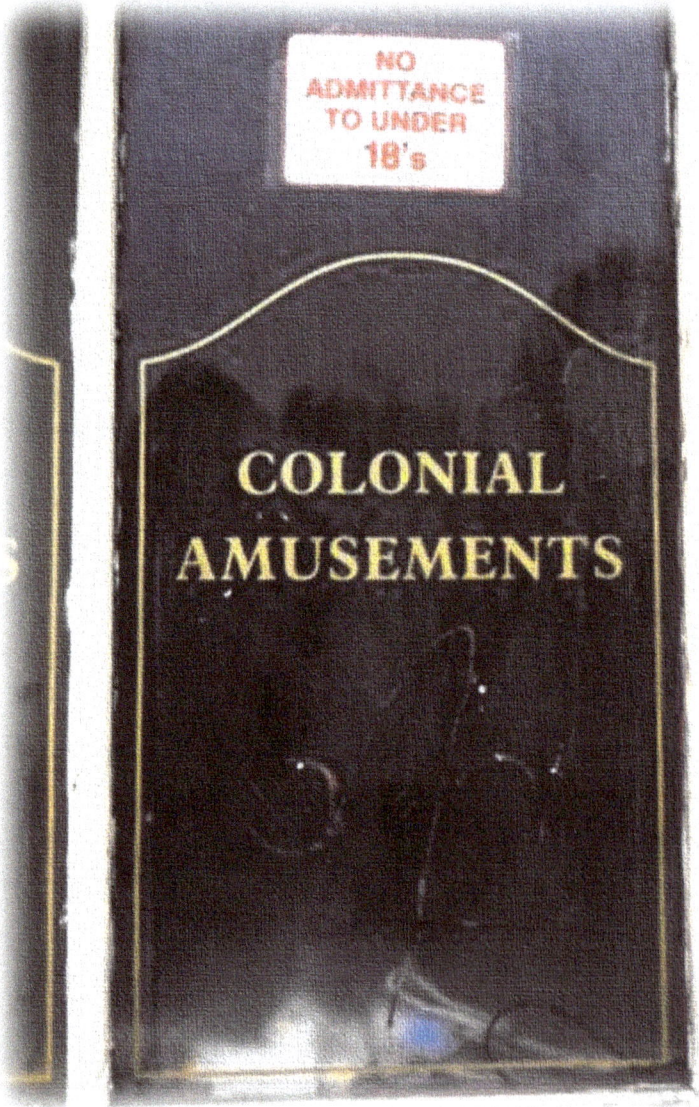

12/ the colonial zombie; the real myth

Who walks?

All of the walks suggested in this book will be inflected, and more, by how you appear to others.

At the end of 'Night', famously, the African American lead character, Ben, sole survivor of those sheltering in the farmhouse, is shot by vigilantes led by Sheriff McClellan – "That's another one for the fire!" From the point of view of the white zombie hunters, race and monstrosity are conflated in the firing of a synapse.

"Who walks?" changes everything. Now you are "zombie"/ "terrorist", now you fit the profile, now you are in the sights of homeland security. Now how do you walk?

Take a walk where you might be misunderstood or misrecognised. Falls Road, Ramallah, a travellers' camp; share a melting continent with a polar bear. For some of you reading this, there might be nowhere else.

In numerous undead products, from the subversive 'Marvel Zombies' to the nostalgic 'Victorian Undead', there are critically distanced nods to the horrors of imperialism: US superheroes rot and predate, Buckingham Palace is decked in the banners of an undead empire. Even in zombie movies set exclusively on localised US terrain a post-colonial self-awareness can emerge: early in the Kentucky-set 'Return of the Living Dead' the foreman of a medical supplies warehouse describes its teaching skeletons: "international treaty, all skeletons come from India... I think there's a skeleton farm over there". Freddy, the new boy, asks "how come?" and we can all take a pretty good guess at why.

However, the colonial undead are more extensively, if less palatably, represented in those 'Euro-zombi' movies of the 1970s and 1980s that sourced their back stories from their countries' ecclesiastical-colonial pasts.

Filmed during the gradual thawing of cultural restrictions in a still authoritarian, cold war Europe, these reactionary cinemas drew their horror not from a predation that followed its own pattern, but one borrowed from skewed depictions of a colonial 'other'. Fuelled by post-colonial fears around the loss of will (political and sexual) in the face of an alien 'old' culture, these movies reanimated imperialist attitudes for modern society. In the 'Blind Dead' series, the rotted corpses of Templar Knights, medieval enforcers for religio-imperial adventures in the Middle East, punish contemporary anxieties about sex, style, gender and power. Re-animating the exotic bodies of plantation workers, Lucio Fulci's zombi movies messily shuffled science with superstition. In place of Romero's democratic cannibal (with all the contradictions that that description implies), the darker recesses of European trash cinema produced a reactionary monster, adding unprecedented litres of gore and lingering close-ups of injuries to filmic essays in colour and tempo. It is disturbing to think that for many audiences these monsters rather than Romero's "blue collar kind of monster" (p.57, Hervey) were, and perhaps still are, the "reigning cultural bad dream" (p.72, Williams) and "mythopoesis of our time" (p.30, Saunders).

Lucio Fulci's 1979 movie 'Zombie Flesh Eaters/Zombi 2' masquerades as a sequel to Romero's 'Dawn'. In its early scenes, and in a final one, its zombies come on very Romero, ordinary looking, the dead *demos* of 'Night', flapping about on an abandoned boat in New York harbour and then massing on Brooklyn Bridge to march on Manhattan. Once the narrative traces the origins of the outbreak to the Caribbean, however, it turns up a rotten colonial history. A re-animated Spanish conquistador emerges from the ground on which a young couple are making out. A punisher like Ossario's unseeing Knights. Against the expansive and dispersed eroticism of the Romero mythos, these ancient monsters are morbidly conflicted; opening up the body's insides in spectacular reds and purples while clamping down on the vital sex of the living. They crawl out of shallow graves, sometimes bald, dry and sculptural, statue-like and desiccated or caked with soft matter (Fulci called them "walking flower pots"), shown to their best effect when defamiliarised. As when Fulci shifted his work from the Caribbean to the US in 'The Beyond' (1981); his skewed depictions of New England and Louisiana, and of an urban modernism infested with European colonial revenants like the 19th-century zombie Dr Freudstein, generated hallucinatory un-places.

Stumbling about, without identifiable signifieds or reliable objective correlatives, these movies, with their free floating symbols and unhinged sequences, at times seem to animate and picture 'pure ideology'.

Ironically, they often invite more radical readings than the crude Marxian metaphors of their more sincere equivalents, digging up the colonial revenant in modern Western narratives and setting it in motion towards old territory. If Romero's 'Dawn' is didactic, then they can be too: "'Zombie Creeping Flesh'... has a message... if we do not feed the Third World then they will come and feed on us" (p.158, Goodall). Their representations of an empty and obliging landscape of 1970s nihilism are prophetic of the shock capitalism and neo-imperialism to come.

The distinctive nature of the camerawork in these movies is significant. There is no harm in reminding ourselves that these movies are not recorded performances, let alone representations with originals, but fantasies constructed through the lens of a machine that can move, root itself, track, pan and zoom. In Romero's 'Night' the filming is documentary-like; a scene where the living dead, relaxed after their attacks, consume body parts is cool, bland and distantly explicit. The camera has a glassy stare. But with Fulci the camera comes zooming in on the viscera again and again, rubbing the audience's noses in the blood and guts. There is little that is restrained about 'Zombie Flesh Eaters' and its ilk, and their grisly carnival-like abandon is a part of their popular impact and success. However, despite their energised morbidity, their excessive gore and body-tearing effects, it is the grue of colonialism that stalks them that is most abject.

Grues are fictional monsters that dwell in darkness; like the zombie, they are born in night. Rarely seen, their presence in the shadows determines access to space. From Fulci, de Ossario, Bianchi, Lenzi, Mattei, D'Amato and their like we get some sense of their shadowiness. They manifest in the melancholic electronic soundtracks of their movies, like broken ventilation systems droning to a halt.

Despite these movies' pretence of modernity, their grues are 'ancient'; their invisibility is testimony to how natural they propose themselves to be. Though the empires have been mostly undone, their grues continue to operate under the black suns of fashion and civilisation; they propose new wars for women's rights, for democracy, for persecuted minorities and in defence of the birthplaces of civilisation. On the Brooklyn Bridge, shuffling down the corridor of a Madrid design house, or invading a TV studio in Rome, their infections and invasions propose themselves as timeless and universal, their bodies can pierce any ground of self-determination from beneath, they permit no alternative.

Walk your city seeking out signs of colonialism; for each historic example (a street called 'Empire Villas', a 'Victoria Hall', a statue of a colonialist) find an equivalent modern neo-colonial grue (orientalist advertising, traditional pantomime narratives, deportations, queues of migrant workers waiting for a white van). The revenants will change all this.

For all the gore and attrition upon their living characters, the movies of the likes of Fulci, de Ossario and others are fetid with nostalgia, a rubbing together of rotting palms at the despatch of the present by the past. As Roger Luckhurst has adroitly pointed out, it is not so much the "history of slavery and colonial dispossession that underpins its origins... [but W]hat is complex about the figure [of the zombie] is often the way this atrocious undertow is at once avowed and disavowed" (p.15). While the revenant of the Euro-zombi often explicitly rises from a colonial history or geography, the movies are often painfully keen to present themselves as having 'up-to-date' content, to be full of fashionable living and young things. Setting the past on the present the movies at once set up a binary of separation – the fashionable present has no connection to, or similarity with, the rotted colonial past – and at the same time wholly infects this new kind of present with a colonial ambience. This is sophisticated spectacularisation. Not surprisingly, as with any economy of the spectacle, these movies perform most blatantly what they set out to hide. In this case, just who they think the monsters are: the victims. Those weak and liberal individualists who dare to break the rules of private behaviour, family, nation and body, who separate themselves from authority and society, who are becoming a new kind of human. Ironically, but significantly, this is most true of the movie to which the 1968 zombie owes most, directed by Ubaldo Ragona and Sydney Salkow, filmed in Rome and Italian-made: 'Last Man on Earth'/'L'ultimo uomo della terra' (1964).

Coming a decade before the wildly coloured Euro-zombis, 'Last Man' has something of the monochrome paranoia that Romero's 'Night' shares with 'Invasion of the Body Snatchers' (1956) and the atomic-zombie movie 'Invisible Invaders' (1959).

Most histories of film zombies have remarked on what the makers of 'Night' helped themselves to from 'Last Man': the sluggish "all messed up" walk of the dead, their regeneration after death (with a familial touch from W. W. Jacobs' 'The Monkey's Paw'), their massing in crowds that focus on a single prey, their pixilated memories, the dread ambience of a deserted funfair, supermarket scenes and 'free' shopping sprees, the ruins of media (the last man, played by an appropriately incongruous Vincent Price, has a movie projector) and the house under siege with arms breaking through its boarded-up windows. What these accounts mostly miss, though, is the moment in 'Last Man' that Romero's *oeuvre* is all the time trying to return to, when the last human survivor discovers that his daytime predations upon the sleeping bodies of nocturnal vampires have in part been a slaughter of a new kind of humanity.

Price is confronted with the meaning of his daily predations, when he meets a young woman. Ruth, who looks human but turns out to be a member of a group of hybrid vampire/humans, a new kind of human, some of whom Price has killed on his daylight staking sprees. His response is horrifying for there not being one. Price's indifference is the climax of the horror. Presented with the consequences of his actions, Price is ready to continue with his genocidal routine the very next day. 'Getting the message across' makes no difference to this everyday monster: "another day to live through... better get started... how many more of these... until they are all destroyed?"

This is, perhaps, the very shadowiest part of the mythos, hidden within all its journeys, no matter how exploratory, escapist or benign, whether it be Ana driving at full speed through the dromologically infected suburbs or Number 9 and Big Daddy leading their undead *dérivistes* from the malevolent city: all these accidental and hyper-sensitised 'explorations' of new territories, or of familiar ones made strange, are shadowplays of a much older, genocidal mission. No wonder Fulci wants to drive us back to it, grind our faces into the grave dirt of it. All our zombie walking is infected by a mission against alien "Life", against that unity which is part being and part thing. This genocidal routine is the discomforting drive of our zombie body; its purest expression is not Bub, Tar Man or Cemetery Zombie, but 'Last Man' Price. The "monster to them". The punisher of the miscegenation of human and other. As Ruth, part human/part vampire, says of and to Price: "you're a legend in the city... many of the people you destroyed were still alive... loved ones of the people in my group". This is what the reactionary and eugenicist Price monster is let loose upon: the human bio's progressive multiplicity.

Beyond revelations about the 'human in the monster' (fragments of memory, agency for an avenging moral fate) and the 'monster in the human' (mostly 'Aunt Sallies' like Sheriff McClellan and his vigilantes), what these reactionary European movies are nudging us towards and then driving us back from with their relentless hordes of prejudice is the return of high capitalism's colonial 'adventures' in the form of our cousins. If we think the "swarms" of refugees fleeing wars that we started are something, then wait until we see the numbers forced out of their lands by the heat dome we have created from the fossil fuels extracted from beneath them.

> *Take one of your solo walks again; this time walk with the 'monster' you are. The pure one; find the purity inside, the what-is-really-me; that part of you that is unique, wholly unlike another. What is your Price? This is the monstrosity, unflinchingly certain in its identity, the fixity that destroys those who are still alive-in-the-world and destroys you-in-the-world from the inside. Your compromise with what cannot be compromised. You can do nothing about it; it is the enemy within. It is what it is.*
>
> *This is a walk about not changing the past; only real monsters do that.*
>
> *Follow living others: birds, bags blown in the wind, helicopters, pylons, cats. Just as Price follows the dog in 'Last Man', leading him, via mountainous piles of earth, monumental steps and a beautiful concrete brutalism, to a first encounter with the vampire/human hybrids. These are the others that can lead you from familiar altars. Rather than sacrifice yourself, making your last stand for the past, be blasphemous, write a new communion, follow Dog and join the hybrid "freaks! mutations!" of the new masses.*

Ruth: "The beginning of any new society is never gentle or charming." That isn't always true...

13/ swarm politics

Things are changing in zombieland. They always are. Despite all appearances, the zombie body is sensitive. Often written and produced by enthusiasts, freeloaders, apprentices and chancers, the narratives, gazes and forms of the zombie product are open to new and wonky impulses: novel fears, drives, technical misfires and sneaky desires.

A case in point would be 'Colin'. Listen to the commentary on the dvd and there is very little to suggest that those involved understood much about how their movie shifts the mythos; its hordes behave more as if in a general social unrest than a cannibal outbreak. When Colin's mother blocks off the windows to the kitchen where he is holed up, we see that the earliest newspaper reports addressed the apocalypse as a social problem. These zombies trip over. They turn on each other, competitively fighting over intestines, their feeding frenzy is like a party suddenly 'getting out of hand'. The zombified Colin is 'mugged' for his trainers by two young black men from the local housing estate transferring the demographic of conservative consumption from that portrayed in 'Zombieland', with high rollers fleeing a casino clutching beer and wads of dollars, to a stereotypical criminally aspirational underclass. The *lair of reactionary intensity* in 'Colin' is similar to the one in the canonically transgressive 'Zombie 108'. 'Colin' puts zombies and humans much closer than usual. Its hyper-exploitation of the zombie, which at first seems to be either torture or sexual violence ("we're going to string him up and then you can do what you want with him") turns out to be an attempt to reunite Colin with his Family. Death squads use the same technology as insurgents in recently invaded countries. They 'blood' their child-soldiers. The final pan is to the sky. Little of this has been typical of previous zombie movies.

Colin's transformation is extended and barely visible. It looks like an early film of subterranean performance art where "loss or semi-loss of light itself skews the founding visibility of performance... rendering the spectatorial act itself into one which is liminal... a hair's breadth from a fall into pitch darkness" (p.70, Barber) or like Mario Bava's 'Black Sunday' when the director "lets the camera roll, filming 'nothing' but the blackness of submerged shadow, at once flat and an infinite depth" (p.107, Thacker). 'Colin' makes the nothingness visible.

The Romero universe-of-the-dead was a remarkably puritanical one; at least in its superficial etiquettes of slaughter, visuality and back story. Such was the overwhelming fear of the dead that sex was the last thing on survivors' minds; though much on the sub-mind of the movies. Long-term relationships rarely held up: "it's not just romantic love but the whole language and social organisation of love and family that is brought into question... everyone is ultimately alone... under an equal compulsion to be 'for themselves'" (p.5, Rutherford). Families were riven. Those participating in unconventional, extra-marital or unlicensed sexual activity on the margins of the Romero mythos (the character Trash dancing naked on graves in 'Return of the Living Dead') were likely to be punished by the plot. For the most part characters heeded the threat and stuck to the immediate business of simple, sincere and ascetic survival, persisting by their willingness to defer gratification until another time (despite the lack of any prospects for one).

A certain 'decency' also prevailed in respect of the living dead. A kind of post-war social democratic consensus operated: violence only when necessary, and, then, rational. The dead reciprocated by (mostly) predating without apparent glee. Not a 'race war' between the living and the living dead then, but un-selfed killings required by the exchange between the twins poles of '*they* are *us*' emotionalism and the social and racial tensions of real societies in meltdown. The movies observed certain pseudo-judicial niceties long after all the judges and juries had been eaten and their courts permanently adjourned.

That is no longer true. While the zombies, despite speeding up, have generally retained a certain level of decency (though in 'Colin' we do see an aggressive feeding corpse growl fiercely at the eponymous zombie-hero, and in 'Remains' [2011] it's the same), the survivors have increasingly abandoned theirs. Even in movies that remain central to the Romero mythos this can be seen: in the casting of zombies in gladiatorial entertainments in 'Land' and 'Tokyo Zombie' (2005), or in Michonne's jawless 'pets' in 'The Walking Dead'. There has, from 'Night' to 'Darkest Day' (2015), been a critical portrayal of any enthusiasm for despatching the dead on the part of state forces or informal gangs of vigilantes, but with films informed increasingly by first person shooter games they have slipped towards sub-Peckinpah ballets of annihilation. Exploitations of the dead, the license to kill what is already dead for the entertainment of audiences, always present in the mythos, are now folded back into the narratives themselves. The morbid 'playfulness' of the scene in the 'Dawn' remake where survivors take potshots at 'celebrity lookalikes' in the zombie horde, swung around Michonne's desperate use of the reanimated corpses of her boyfriend and his best friend as camouflage from zombies and protection from humans, marks a shift towards a colonial exploitation similar to that at work in the early Caribbean-based zombie movies of the 1930s and 1940s. The Restoration-set 'Defoe 1666' and 'Defoe: Queen of the Zombies', with their massive treadmills driven by the living dead (called "reeks", "stenches" or "pretenders"), critically forefront this hyper-exploitation of the living dead and draw connections with the real 17th-century trade in Irish and Africans slaves.

Two recent movies have distilled this tendency in a way that sucks in other misogynies and misanthropies to make poisonous cocktails: 'Wyrmwood' and Taiwan's first zombie movie 'Zombie 108' /'Z-108 qi cheng'. In both these movies there is a making over of sexuality as inevitably violent and morbid, accompanied by an intense exploitation of the zombie character. Since 'Night' the living dead have been destroyed by survivors; where they were experimented upon, as in 'Day', no matter how flakily, some pretext of study and information gathering was proffered. In both 'Zombie 108' and 'Wyrmwood', such niceties are dispensed with and there is a return to a colonial-style hyper-exploitation – "A THOUSAND PER CENT INCREASE IN THE PROFITS OF THE ROYAL RESURRECTION COMPANY... THANKS TO SUPPLYING REEKS TO THE COLONIES" brags Colonel Blood in 'Defoe: Queen of the Zombies' – with the clear echoes of slavery already clunkily at work in Hammer's costume-horror 'Plagues of the Zombies' (1966) and in 'The Zombie Farm' (2009); each with its own return of 'old' magic. Once so stirringly bleak, ascetic and inspiringly dread, the mythos is struggling to avoid complete entanglement in everyday economy, commerce and an exploitable and 'uncivilised' world characterised by 'ancient superstition'. In the back stories of these movies the apocalypse stretches back further than one might imagine, to a normality that has long been apocalyptic; expressed far more starkly than any horror movie or comic could by the widely publicised image of European holidaymakers sunbathing beside the corpse of a drowned refugee from the wars in North Africa.

We are losing that oddly invigorating revolutionary morbidity that George Romero introduced us to in 1968, but we are also getting closer to the 'them' that are us, and they are getting closer to the 'us' that is them. This 'over-familiarisation' of what was once de-familiarised, is captured (literally) in scenes of sexual, labour and energy exploitation in 'Wyrmwood'. The reanimated are strapped onto and plumbed into car engines, fuelling them with their noxious breath; a mechanisation of the dead similar to the character Robert Hooke's development of cyborg cannibal corpses ('clockpunks') in 'Defoe: Queen of the Zombies'. The dead are exploited just like any other fossil fuel. In 'Zombie 108' (in similar scenes to those in the mobile lab in 'Wyrmwood') a cadaverous human predator has zombies working on a treadmill powering his flat, while he seeks out and sexually abuses women, human and zombie. To Romero's bright overlaying of the living and the dead – "[A]t the end of the film ['Land']... the evolved zombies... seem to be drafting the plans for a non-repressive marriage between civilisation and instincts" [p.208, Clark]) – this is the dark side. Here nothing has changed – like the two gamblers fleeing the overrun casino at the beginning of 'Zombieland', not only do "the living continue to operate within the discourses of the old world – consumption, competition, consumerism" (p.71, Deslandes & Adamson), but they also seek to take advantage of the disaster by spreading it further through the dismemberment of social organisation and public space; gambling everything on the invisible hand of the 'free market' (ready to reach up even from the grave) and the efficacy of their own groping for possession.

This new 'survivor' reflects (analytically in 'What's Left Of Us', crudely in 'Zombie 108') an intensification of exploitation in the face of climate change, global economic recession and debt, the dissolution of leftist collectivity, and a ratcheting up of the backlash against women in the interests of threatened male privileges and aspirations for a final theological solution to the 'problem' of different bodies: "Are dead social forms merely sleeping and waiting their moment to reawaken? What if women are once again sexual commodities to be traded by men, and men are once more a band of brothers cowering under the threat of a primal father?" (p.7, Rutherford) It may be intended as humorous, but there is something chilling about the "exemption from the United Nations Declaration of Human Rights" in regard to the treatment of the living dead in Sean T. Page and Ian Moores' *Zombie Survival Manual* (2013).

This particular 'Manual' advocates the use of zombies as fuel (haven't they watched 'Return'?), as labour on treadmills and as beasts of burden. Such treatments of the mythos as pseudo-reality normalise end times theologies, hyper-exploitation, a psychotic lack of empathy, gun ownership and a fear of everything 'other'.

> *Walk as if exhausted. Make plans for escapes from violent lairs and act on them.*

The most obvious interpretation of the zombie, as exploited worker, has returned with a vengeance. No longer a distanced critique of social relations enforced by the state and corporations, the metaphor is woven inextricably into character narratives, beliefs, drives and super-objectives. It implicates us as viewers and readers and imaginary participants in a neo-liberal exploitation of everyday life to which there is no alternative, a post-world where what is past is the financial Big Bang, privatisation of major industries, the growth of hedge funds, stock market speculation on the space above buildings, Enron trading in its own profits, the leveraging of Lehman Brothers and the general ideological and economic victory (despite their political and military defeats) of the Neo-Cons. In other words, these movies show you "how real abstractions work on real bodies... when seemingly spectral shifts in the global architecture... touch earth and produce real consequences" (p.80, Williams).

More recently, the extreme violence against black citizens and the impact made by the rancid and inane populism of Donald Trump in the US, the begrudging and hostile responses by many Western European governments to the Syrian refugee crisis (and the attempt by some to take advantage of it to promote their previously frustrated wish to bomb Syria) are driving a minority of people to embrace socialist politicians and to question just how liberal the 'liberal democracies' might be. The very best people, those who volunteer their time to charities and community groups, have increasingly discovered that their agency has been transformed; that tax breaks for the rich and targeted cuts in public funding and their matched substitution by volunteer activity has turned them into volunteers for banks and billionaires. These good people are abolished, along with virtue, and returned in a wholly different identity, though nothing they did changed from one year to the next. This is zombification. This is why even some rather surprising individuals are beginning to re-think a history in which equality, access and life with both dignity and self-determination (even though, up to this moment, not to them) have always been denied to many by democracies that favour private profits over the interests of the 'horde'; begging the riddle posed by Ta-Nehis Coates: "how to erect a democracy independent of cannibalism". (p.105, Coates)

In 'Colin' a female survivor fleeing a mass attack is ushered into the 'safety' of a cellar with the words: "you're perfectly safe with me". It is a harem of corpses. Remember: the people who are 'saving' you from these disasters (Tories paying back the debt, and so on) are the people who delivered you up to them in the first place.

Make a new walk sensitising yourself to 'lairs of reactionary intensity', to labs and cellars (see pp.10-15, Smith, 2015).

Distrust apparent havens. Finding your way to somewhere in the apocalyptic labyrinth is more dangerous than getting lost in it.

If you are a stranger, refugee, immigrant, outsider, prisoner, unemployed or disabled, retired or without sufficient savings to play a significant role in consumption, keep a look out for what Jack Halberstam calls 'zombie humanism'; that dehumanisation by industrialised and institutionalised assistance of those who do not fit with normative definitions of what 'living' is, transferring humanity and agency from receiver to giver.

Inside the institutions and cultures of 'zombie humanism' work the informal monsters, hidden in plain sight, vicious operators who exude an oppressive charm, oddness and recklessness. They propose themselves as outrageously liberal, sensual and ironically deferential. They are the opposite in each case; they are philosophical zombies, looking human but without qualia, propagating illiberality, convention, sterility, coldness and reverence under the guise of mad fun.

In 'The Road' (2009) based on a Cormac McCarthy novel, a film with similarities to the Romero zombie movie, a father and son come upon a group of naked wretches being kept as food in a locked basement. One of these lunches grabs the father's leg, trying to persuade him to stay and share their suffering: "wait, wait, you get used to it!" This is not the cellar of 'Psycho' with its rampant 'id' trying to get loose; this is repression, making horror acceptably routine, part of the working of the lair of reactionary intensity: even those who have nothing to gain by your exploitation, and on whose "real bodies" are working "real abstractions", will try to suck you in. Such lairs distil the living dead mythos of exploitation, slavery, de-humanisation and unrestricted consumption; sites of a violent drive expressed without conscience or empathy which Evan Calder Williams detects as constituent of the fiction itself: "a secret communal fantasy of nastiness toward our fellow human... the zombie film lets us bare our open secret and celebrate in it" (pp.83-4).

Zombie walking offers very little in the way of social action; it steps back from that spectacle. Yet it may be the prelude to your taking action against the predators at large in your streets dressed in priest's robes, clone suits or celebrity bling. You might be surprised by what you can detect while staying within the mask of the implacable zombie, traipsing abjectly and with no apparent reason or value, attracting neither attention nor desire. By learning to put your focus aside, short-circuiting the spectacle by the to-the-sideness of your characterless performance; yet ready to snap up information when those around you are recklessly indiscreet.

Steve Hanson has called for a dropping of occult psychogeography in favour of a materialist exploration (see p.68, Smith, 2015). Can't we have both? A materialist examination with the tools of absurd fiction? Paul Virilio protests that where "once the polis inaugurated a political theatre, with its agora and its forum, now there is only a cathode-ray screen, where the shadows and spectres of a community dance amid their processes of disappearance" (p.386, Virilio); the blank body of zombie walking is a screen that we can turn inside out, walking its spectres back into real places. Looking *for*, rather than at, monsters.

Walk in symbol, pleasure, performance, display. Combine the walk of 'zombie solidarity' (which will always have some bias towards sincerity and ascetics) with its partial opposite:

theatricality, trans-everything, betweenness and transgression, a vivid colour palate, skin covered and skin bared. Make an anti-sincerity, anti-ascetic, anti-Romero walk; a chance to throw off the mythos for a while and remind yourself that all such fictions, like all representations, have only a strictly limited efficacy, only as good as the quality of the rejections that they lead you to.

14/ the schism

Pat Mills and Leigh Gallagher's post-Great Fire of London (or '666) 'Defoe' comics are set in a powerfully ambiguous alternative/non-alternative history; the restoration of the monarchy has taken place and the last remnants of the leftist forces from the Civil War work together with the establishment and "the lowest of the low" to fight off zombie hordes from both and no sides of the past conflict. Forget that arcane controversy over zombies walking or zombies running; these can fly!

They have a certain demonic power; yet there is nothing exotic about the magic that empowers them, it is strictly contextualised to the beliefs of the historical time. Mills's fiction neatly condenses the ambiguities of the English Civil War, in which aristocrats often fought for Parliament and new-bourgeois merchants likewise for the king; a conflict that contradicts the popular Marxian interpretation of a bourgeois revolution, and is more amenable to the picture drawn by Mills and Gallagher of a war of ideas (theological and political) fought through the prism of local and selfish interests. These comics are far from backward looking despite their historical setting, describing the same milieu as that deftly anatomised by Naomi Klein as the shock doctrine of disaster capitalism. "TURNING THE DISASTER OF '666 INTO A GREAT ECONOMIC OPPORTUNITY", as one character puts it. Crucial to our not being able to do anything about the machine of this doctrine is the role of a disastrous schism that runs through the Western left, rooted originally in religion, and from which it cannot shake itself (in fact when it tries it only shakes itself apart), and which originates from the same milieu as the 'Defoe' narratives.

During the Civil War and Republic of 1640-1660 the rightwards elements in the English revolution expressed themselves through the authoritarianism of Oliver Cromwell and his supporters and their suppression of the Roundhead left's policies for radical democratic reforms and wealth re-distribution. These leftist elements were only successful in implementing their most Puritan policies: closing theatres, pulling down maypoles and generally suppressing intellectual, 'pagan' and 'Popish' pleasures. Here the schism opens up in the 'English Left' – between pleasure and equity – that then infects multiple socialisms.

The result of this lopsideness, at the cultural scale, is Left-Puritanism; espoused and lived day-to-day by a large Leveller faction within the Parliamentary army – a faction hunted down and decapitated by the army's high command through 1647 to 1649. The character Defoe a survivor from this faction; rough, fiercely egalitarian and ascetic in spirit, speaking freely of "sin" and quick to identify carnal, conceptual, perceptual and aesthetic pleasures as effete and Cavalier-reactionary. This is the flaw in Defoe, the tragic hero, who fights the hordes of dead, the bodies of both his friends and foes, for the future of human and 'godly' life, reluctantly allied to the servants of the reanimated English throne and various hangmen, paedophiles and pressgangers. Part of Defoe's tragic strength is to make this compromise without any effect upon his personal convictions; he lacks the dead horde's capacity to gobble up everything. His dry subjectivity, the clear and transparent intuition that serves him so well in combat with the dead, is what makes him, like 'Last Man' Price, yet another radical corpse in politics; advocating change and yet unable to change.

Unfortunately, the Western left has largely followed Defoe, capitulating freedom and rich subjectivity to various post-Thatcherite/Reaganite neo-liberalisms that have been remarkably successful given how socially conservative were their figureheads; but the richness of an ideology lies not in its consistency or reality, but in its phantasmagoric resonance. Something that few leftish thinkers (Stephen Duncombe and Jean Baudrillard, perhaps) grasp. Despite the diversionary fireworks in 'Land' or Dr Logan's assertion that the zombies "can be fooled... tricked into being good little girls and boys, the same way we were tricked into it", ideology is not primarily about diversion or subterfuge. It operates by openly inscribing itself in flesh, in the visual, and in desires and appetites that evade analysis.

Dr. Logan makes no great discoveries about what drives the zombie, but his evisceration of the dead, and his morphing of human corpses into incentives, sits alongside other ideological flesh-makings such as the Tuskegee Syphilis Study's deliberate and covert infection of African Americans, Fluoridisation (benign or not), the secret spraying of Winnipeg with zinc cadmium sulphide, the CIA's experimentation with LSD on unconsenting individuals, and many, many more equally disturbing projects. Plus the food industry in general (a cursory check of what is for sale as nourishment where corporate ownership is most intense makes the predation of the living dead look relatively harmless). This was always part of the pattern; a dance of bio-ideology (60% of food energy fed to livestock who then reduce that down to 15%, but add huge floods of effluent and profits), skipping easily between control and license across the borderland of crime and legislation, with the latter often on top of the former. Who will ever forget the wonderful carnival of meat diversity, with horse so ubiquitous? Almost everyone.

> *Choreographer and academic Victoria Hunter has written about a 'pedestrian rule' that dancers can use during improvisations to engage an integrated and anti-dualist idea of personhood. If, during an improvisation, a dancer begins to "feel a sense of disconnection with the movement exploration scores leading to the production of movement content which was inauthentic... The pedestrian rule enabled the dancers to openly acknowledge their disconnection and to simply walk, pause, observe and take time to reconnect with the site and the other bodies in the site" (p.190, Hunter) .*

> *Wait until you experience a moment similar to the disconnection described here, a fraying or splitting of personhood, a turning of the self into multiple threads, an alienation from place, and then "walk, pause, observe and take time" but rather than use the pedestrian rule as a means to return to authentic connection, prolong the disconnection, and walk in the ruins of your personhood and through the disconnections of space until they (personhood and place) come back to you, in a new connection.*

15/ they came to fuck the dead back to life

'LA Zombie' (2010), directed by Bruce LaBruce, puts into practice, sexually, the post-apocalyptic dictum of Margaret Killjoy's that it is "only by working with your community (and I mean community to mean 'the people who live near you' and not 'the people I like and go to the same conventions as') that you might find the way to meet your needs" (p.4, Killjoy). Not many people are likely to attend conventions with LaBruce's hero, a luminescent alien zombie, his face erupting in a cluster of enormous incisors, wreaking havoc upon the oppressor and then reviving them with his penis, who may be the hallucination of a homeless man. But then again...

Among other things Bruce LaBruce makes gay porn movies. 'LA Zombie' deploys the repetitions, anonymities and predictable scenario outcomes of hardcore porn. LaBruce proposes the corporeal excesses and de-subjectivisations of zombie-human and human-group-zombie sex as an erotic collectivism against a violent, self-obsessed, greedy and exclusive neo-liberalism. The sex is not separated from the scenarios, but integral to the meaning of the film: neo-liberalism is death. Non-normative, non-reproductive sex is new life.

Reanimation's agent for this new life emerges not from theoretical conviction, nor from the kind of disenfranchised and disenchanted emotional heroism that LaBruce brought to life in 'Otto: up with dead people!' (2008), but from nature: the alien rises from the sea. He moves about on the edges of non-productivity; from food queues (where he is subjected to the 'zombie-humanism' of the attendants) to the concrete expanses of the Los Angeles River and gang disputes. It is as though LaBruce has taken the infamous 'bath salts' re-categorisation by commercial and social media of a tragic psychosis as a zombie event and turned it back on the horror genre; reanimating its phantasmagoric representations with a perverse realism.

This zombie's rootlessness is significant; comparable with 'drifting'. As a wanderer he can open up different void spaces in the city, but he has no destination, simply looking for some 'place to go'. Alien he may be, but no alien-invader. Despite his shape-shifting magic, he is melancholic, at times swept along in the trajectories of the city, its lights flashing by as dollarscapes emerge from the twinkling dark of the big city night. The alien-zombie's transformative agency, effective through connection rather than ejaculation, relies upon the confluences of more affordant stages than LA's skylines and unstopping freeways. His power is far from universal; he is reliant on the excessive overflowing of other bodies to meet his own. He cannot shoulder a general hope, there are no neo-Hegelian forces of determination at work on behalf of this pop-culture icon, he emerges from collective suffering and injustice, but, contra-zombie, he is always subjective, hallucinated and extraordinary. He weeps for the dead he has revived; he resurrects but he changes little. He digs in the grave of LAW but finds nothing there to revive.

Hopeful innovations in the mythos like LaBruce's Los Angeles zombie are single threads, the beginnings of journeys, signposts that have to be realised by walking their walk, continuing their predation or carrying their infection. A similarly broken cord is the new Barbara (her name subtly changed from the 'Barbra' of 1968.) At the end of Tom Savini's 1990 remake of 'Night of the Living Dead' something remarkable occurs; so genre-shifting that I have yet to find any critic who has paid it any attention. Reviewers have fixated on the variations the movie plays on the character of Ben. The unplanned, supposedly 'colour-blind' casting of an African American for this part in the first 'Night' transformed the meaning of that film, charging its conflicts with contemporary resonance. In the Savini remake, Ben is less competent, more conflicted. Trying to make sense of the changes to his character, hypnotised by the meta-cinema, it is easy to miss the massive subversion of the mythos that Savini and his screenwriter Romero have conjured in the moments after Ben's death.

In this 1990 'Night', Ben becomes zombie and is shot (as in 1968) by redneck vigilantes who have accompanied Barbara back to the farmhouse. But then another figure looms out of the darkness. It is a living, surviving Harry Cooper. Barbara shoots him in the head, and then, in a twisted reference to Ben's death in the original 'Night', she passes Cooper off to the vigilantes as living dead: "another one for the fire". Kevin Wetmore Jr. describes this killing as "cold", the moment, in his judgement, transforming the film from "exploitation movie... into reactionary feminist film: the ends justify the means if it brings about social change and female empowerment" (p.62). What follows, however, suggests something far more radical than that. Already, in her killing of the divisive Cooper, Barbara has taken responsibility for human society over and beyond its defence from an outside attack. She has begun a "terror" inside. Now, she exits the farmhouse, standing on the stoop to watch the rednecks piling the bodies high on the bonfire. The film is almost over. The live action, as in the original, switches to a set of stills.

It took no great act of imagination to read the final still images in the 1968 movie as evocative of lynchings and attacks on Civil Rights marches. It is even easier, then, to read Savini's final sequence of stills as a simple repetition of the original movie. But this is to ignore the stills of Barbara's face and eyes, her gaze and the intensity of her look, interposed between the stills of the rednecks and the bonfire. Attend closely to those images and it is hard not to ask yourself, as I think the movie is nudging us ask: "what is Barbara thinking?"

Much more of a feminist change of scale than her character's shift from reserve and uncertainty to adroit agency, it is this emergence of interiority that unpeels the film. Despite her execution of the socially corrosive Cooper, this is no guilty introspection – this is a utopian introspection. Barbara is looking *through and beyond* that experience and her responsibility to Life, to the rednecks' bonfire of corpses. There is no disgust in her face, but rather a stare of recognition, understanding, even empathy. Not, with the living dead, but with the real aliens of the zombie mythos: the white working class.

Romero and Savini may well have been wary of making too obvious a statement that might have been interpreted as supportive of Confederate flag waving, Red State fascism; indeed at the end of his more formalistic and cynical – "the more voices there are, the more spin there is" – 'Diary of the Dead' (2007), Romero reverts to the politics of 'Night' by ending on the furious eyes of a female zombie face, partly blown away with all of its body by "a couple of hometown Joes". Re-viewing the scenes from the 1990 movie, after Barbara's initial walking away from the farmhouse, particularly when watched through the prism of Margaret Killjoy's statement about community being the people close by rather than the people you meet at conventions, it is hard not to more fully appreciate what a leap the movie makes. From the nihilistic claustrophobia of the farmhouse with its inverted conflicts of status, race and class to the carnivalesque and efficient seeing off of the zombie threat by a rural working class.

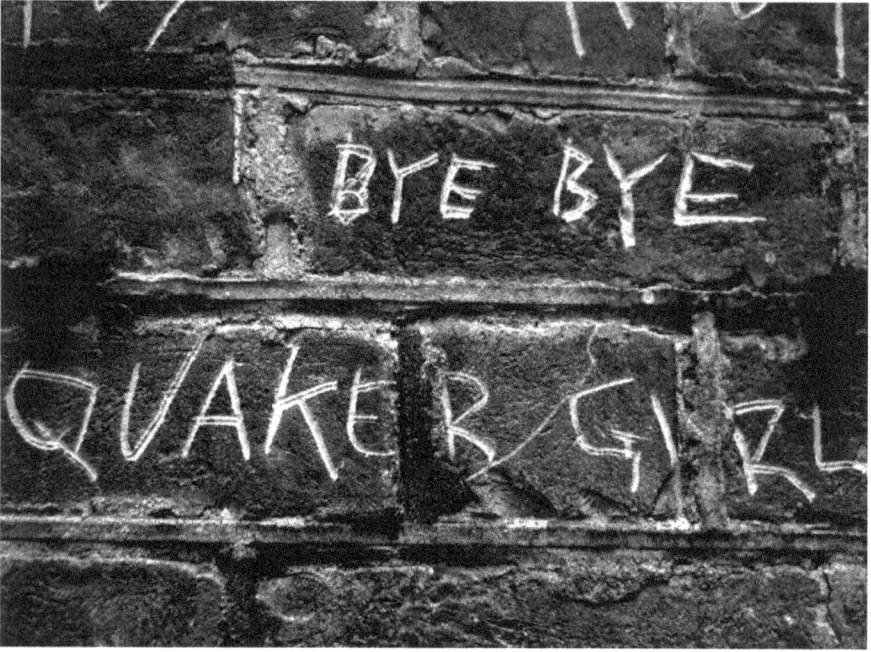

For the audience there is a powerful sense of relief, of a shifting of power, of sunlight and colour (very different to the continuation of monochrome across night to daytime in the original). What had seemed like an overwhelming existential threat to the bunch of squabbling, mostly middle class know-it-alls in the farmhouse, now turns out to be at worst an irritant and at best an entertainment for those familiar with getting their hands dirty. Barbara, now looking like a Ripley or a Sarah Connor, has dispensed not only with the prim dress and shirt in which we first met her in the cemetery, but also with her prim attitudes. She observes the various phantasmagoric sideshows – the shooting at strung up zombies, a drunk fighting a zombie in an improvised ring, the hot dog stands and beer sales – with a bemused but not wholly contemptuous gaze. Her reaction is ambiguous; her statement "we're them, they're us" (similar to Peter's in the original 'Dawn' that "they're us, that's all" which clearly refers to the zombies) may not refer to zombies at all, but instead to the working class hunters, equally in shot and focus, who 'toy' with captured zombies, "demonstrate a considerable sense of community and pleasure" (p.61, Wetmore) and greet Barbara with "what in the name of Great Jupiter's balls are you doing out here alone, little lady?" Her look is not one of existentialist rumination on being and identity, but one of class solidarity against a rapacious, but removable scourge.

These final sequences stage what the situationists called the 'merchant-showman economy' and in the midst of it all, the awakening of its nemesis: subjectivity recognising its own general desires, the realisation that "the disappearance a civilisation generally doesn't take the form of a chaotic war of all against all" and that, instead, "the decomposition of this world... creates openings for other ways of living, including... carnival" (p.37, The Invisible Committee). At last, in the most unpromising of fictionalised circumstances, comes a hint of the possibility of putting aside apocalypse.

So, to summarise the revolutionary programme of Savini's 'Night': Interiority. Carnival. Future.

In the two final stills, intercut with images of the rednecks stacking the bonfire with the dead, Barbara looks as though she might be reviewing troops, thinking to herself 'if this force was ever to direct itself against its real enemies...'

> *Let your wandering take you into the spaces that are 'alien' for you, walk 'off the planet', seek out any places that you may find unnervingly different. Even if that means boringly different: swathes of suburbia just as much as the dangerous streets or the heterotopias of the markets, diverse strips and public squares. If you genuinely fear these spaces because they pose a physical threat to you, then there is something wrong with the spaces, but if you fear them because they challenge your idea of what space is or should be, then take your differences for a walk there; as they inscribe on you, you inscribe on them.*

With Barbara's cultural shift and the LaBruce zombie's disruption of the margins of Los Angeles pointing to possible directions, the mythos as a whole, in both its dire reaction as well as its weird illumination, requires that it stretch itself increasingly across cultural and class boundaries if it is to have anything further to say about how the world ends.

16/ dark souls

A woman jogger is pursued through shady woods by a masked man clutching an electric power drill and dressed in what looks to be a Guantanamo Bay orange detainee uniform. Dragging her to the ground, the man proceeds to drill into her head. After the recovery of her dead body, the young woman, Johanna, revives on a hospital trolley and makes her way home, where she appears to vegetate in front of her computer while her father, Morten, makes dinner. With echoes of 'The Shining' (there are many nods to iconic movies in this meta-film) she types "help me" again and again. By the time her father finally grasps that this is something other than everyday non-communication, the young woman has begun to vomit a thick black liquid.

These are the opening, hackneyed, misogynistic and unpromising scenes of the Norwegian movie, 'Mørke Sjeler' (2010). Literally "Dark Souls", the film was released on dvd as 'Zombie Driller Killer'! It is mostly shot as a gloomy and gritty modern Scandinavian noir, but every now and again it stumbles queasily across other genre terrains. Its odd stylistic and narrative assemblage set against a realist city, and the film's uncertainty about itself, make it a perversely apposite, and almost wholly unrecognised (the title didn't help) signpost to a new kind of zombie: a petrochemical zombie with a particularly nomadic line of flight, "a lubricant, something that eases narration and the whole dynamic towards the desert... the undercurrent of all narrations, not only the political but also that of the ethics of life on earth" (p.19, Negarestani).

Walk like oil, thickly. Walk with viscosity. Think like oil.

In 2015 the walking artist Jess Allen walked for a week carrying energy-saving light bulbs as gifts with which to begin conversations. This was part of her 'Tracktivism'; she walks quiet public footpaths and encounters other path users as a way to generate discussions around ecological, social and energy issues. What gift or obligation could you carry to begin an oil-based conversation about how best to end the world? Be a remedy for the empty streets.

In the city there are soon multiple victims of drillings to the head, all reviving and prodigiously vomiting the strange oil-like liquid. Faced by an intransigent cop and doctors who struggle to make a diagnosis of his daughter's zombie-like symptoms, music-teacher Morten turns sleuth and, with the virtually comatose Johanna in tow, follows clues to a factory where orange-clad workers come and go. Tailing one of these workers, Morten witnesses him drill into the head of another victim and the arrival of an older, authoritative man in old-fashioned clothes, who hands over a jar of dark substance to be inserted into the wound.

In step with recent hyper-exploitations of the living dead, the unusual zombies of 'Mørke Sjeler' are farmed for chemical production. At home, which is now carpeted in plastic sheeting, Johanna produces copious amounts of black liquid. She is, literally, bringing up the issue of oil – with its lubricated politics, chemistry and ecology – directly into the space of the motherless family; filling an 'empty space' that is packed with inhibitions and denials. Morten (who we see filling his car's petrol tank with an empty zombie-like expression on his face, the consumed consumer) is abruptly brought to investigate an oil 'issue' that combines an energy crisis in his family, bio-politics and the power of private capital. Narrowly avoiding being drilled in the head at the mysterious factory, Morten meets a homeless man camped on its perimeter who tells him how, many years previously, he had been a diver for the company.

Drilling for new oil fields, he and the other divers worked long hours, tortured with dizziness and dreams of drowning. The sea was a phantasmagoria. The diver recounts how a colleague had panicked 300 feet down, swimming without pause to the surface. This diver had vomited oil, his face was "empty... eaten" and he cried out: "I've seen The Darkness! It's inside me!"

The diver's tale evokes Thomas Gold's theory of a non-biological, non-fossil origin for oil. According to Gold, oil emerges from much deeper in the earth than where it is found, formed from randomised molecules that are sweated out from rocks under extreme heat picking up organic elements from a "deep hot biosphere" far beneath the Earth's surface. It is a deeper, darker, more lively birth of oil; a denial of oil as dead fossil. The Iranian speculative realist, rational universalist and theory-fictionist Reza

Negarestani uses Gold's theory to evoke the "deeply Chthonic Thingness of petroleum, the Blob. To grasp oil as a lube is to grasp earth as a body of different narrations being moved forward by oil." Negarestani seeks to shift the myth of capitalism from the light of an upwardly seeking progress to the beating "heart of gloopy darkness", in which "petroleum is a terrestrial replacement of the onanistic self-indulgence of the Sun or solar capitalism. Earth dismantles the hegemony of the Sun on a subterranean (blobjective) level" (p.19).

This is a revolutionary gothic, which 'Mørke Sjeler' is quite incapable of containing, eventually falling back on tired tropes: Johanna vomiting oil on her friend Maria who is thus infected, the petrol-zombies in the hospital rising as a horde to cluster on a consultant, mayhem in the city. But we can forget the film and its failings; a thriller is incapable of containing the terror necessary to expunge its horror. Its radical gothic cannot be turned around now. It has welcomed the stickiness of oil into our nightmares of home and begun replacing the sentimental lakes of gore in zombieland with a far deeper biological darkness: "there is no darkness in the world which has not its image in oil" (p.19). At the end of the film, Johanna and Maria, now covered in black oil, have almost completely disappeared into the luminal darkness of an unlit hallway, morphing into performance art. This is a quite different horror from the usual visions of 'peak oil', "the annihilationist and nihilistic capitalism of the Sun" (p.19) and the last barrel of passive, dead, fossil fuel. And quite different from a zombie apocalypse that draws its effectiveness from its failure to propose an alternative. The darkness in Morten and Johanna's hallway is alive. It emerges from an alien life deep below and within our home; an extremophile that is a "[N]arrative organizer... a singular anorganic body with its own agendas" to which the powerful ("Bush and Bin Laden" [both, perhaps significantly, disposed of now in its narratives]) "are obviously petropolitical puppets convulsing along the chthonic stirrings of the blob" (p.20). Not Gaia, but Blob. Not global, but corporeal. The Blob in us, not the airy, sunny goddess 'out there' somewhere on the astral planes, but the darkness brought into our living room; the nothingness within.

Walk like a gloopy Blob. Let things stick to you. Take some string to tie to yourself the things you find. If you 'bump into' a friend or stranger stick with them for a while.

In the daylight, walk as if it was night. Carry a lighted candle or a torch and search for the darkness.

Walk under the bright lights of your night time city, but make your way only in shadows.

Speak to yourself of things which have no place in your experience. Things which you will never experience, cannot experience: the heat and flow of the Earth's core, quantum entanglement, making ice sculptures on Triton, exalting with larks, the elemental bentness of space, "attack ships on fire off the shoulder of Orion", striking a match on a jelly.

Walk as an alien in your own universe.

Find the darkness and 'chat it up'. Take it home to meet the darkness there.

17/ the ancient dead in ourselves – the ecological zombie

It is easy to ignore the origins of the fictional zombie holocaust; the products themselves don't seem that interested in them. At the genesis of the modern zombie in Romero's 'Night' is a tale of a crashed satellite that I once batted away with the words "scream and you'll miss it". Characters in the various Romero sequels have occasionally reached for a religious obfuscation (most famously "when there's no more room in hell, the dead will walk the Earth"), but the significance of the satellite event is never directly refuted, simply befogged.

Other living dead movies begin with chemical spills, nuclear malfunctions and laboratory accidents, while narratives like Maureen F. McHugh's short story 'The Naturalist' (2011) simply describe a confusion of circulating rumours without attempting to identify which is the real cause.

More recently new narratives about extraterrestrial origins have begun to appear. In 'Wyrmwood' the dead rise after a meteor shower, in 'Marvel Zombies' it all begins with "a flash in the sky", in 'Victorian Undead: Sherlock Holmes vs Zombies!' (2010) after a comet enters the Earth's atmosphere, and similarly in 'Defoe 1666' (2009). In these variations on the first origin in 'Night' the implication is clear: while the mythos gives it almost no importance, somewhere long ago in the back story of the 1968 zombie, this is an alien invasion. Not one where humanoid pilots in nuts and bolts saucers land on the White House lawn, but an invasion by non-sentient matter.

The full extent of the consequences of this importing of alien variable probabilities and dis-equilibriums to the Earth are often less than clear, but generally one of the first to emerge, as Simon Bacon writes of Richard Matheson's *I Am Legend* (the source for the source for Romero's 'Night'), is when "the symbiotic bond is broken between the planet and its inhabitants" (p.154). This breaking, however, is also a reconnecting to a much older symbiosis that was philosophically broken by the rift within Descartes' dualism, separating mind from body (a dualism sometimes

123

demonstrated literally in zombie movies). Now, however, the dust of dead stars, from which our bodies are mostly constituted, is beginning to reinstate its singularity.

As Dylan Trigg suggests, it is perhaps not surprising that in a cosmos "teeming with stasis, the body resists being naturalised as a part of the order of things, instead positioning itself as an excess or reminder of a time when 'the cosmos once *was* alive'" (p.37). This same stasis reappears in the body of the zombie: "the fossilised remains of a life beyond experience, but nevertheless constitutive of life" (p.28). So, when Robert Saunders describes the conflicts between zombies and humans as "about terrain as much as they are about bodies" (p.30) he means more than he intends to; for the conflict is not over possession or control, but for a claim to the *matter* of the cosmos itself.

The impossible energy of the living dead is a looping back, beyond the genesis story of its own mythos, to fasten on the oldest corpses in the cosmos; the cold stars.

It is possible that even life on Earth, not simply its materials, began elsewhere in the universe. In Reza Negarestani's strange novel-cum-theory *Cyclonopedia*, a character speculates on oil as "not of the Earth, but of the Outside, planted here as a xeno-chemical Insider" (p.72). In 'Mørke Sjeler' the scenes of Morten within the factory are unmistakable echoes of Val Guest's 'Quatermass 2' (1957) in which silos built for synthetic food production secretly house massive extraterrestrial bio-forms. The main character, Quatermass, dons a whole body suit as a disguise (just as Morten does in the factory) to view the feeding of the vegetable-aliens.

What the disguised Morten witnesses, however, is a literal 'black mass', "archaic slithering rites (Petro-Masonism and its trans-historical tentacles)" (p.19).

Whether or not we are all xenomorphs, actually or metaphorically or both, the materials that make up our bodies have come incredible distances to become us, and are very, very old. They have been formed, pulverised and fused by staggeringly powerful forces; incomparably greater than those that in 1985 uprooted gravestones and felled the trees which had loomed over the cemetery in 'Night'.

Is that the energy that powers the infection of the zombie's bite?

Our deep biological history is not something that we can easily acquire, either empirically or comprehensively. Too much of the evidence is missing. Instead, it re-arrives to us in hallucinations and visions, in stories of things falling from the sky, and most importantly perhaps from a dim sense that the immense tomb of the universe, through which we make our way, is also in us, that it "already constitutes the structure of the subject in the first place... [our] identity... previously thought to be comprised largely of personal memories, is in fact marked by a... prehistory of violence... implicated in the concept of life itself" (p.34, Trigg).

When Max Brooks writes of the inadequacy of conventional warfare against "an enemy that has no 'life' to end" (p.xiii, 2004) he is not describing the living dead – sufficient head shots put an end to them – he is describing inanimate things in general.

> *Next time you are inside a big system – a crowd, a swimming baths, a factory or office block, a sports stadium, a cathedral mass, an election meeting – walk in relation to its subtle wrinkles of energy, surrender to any tiny gravitational pulls towards its non-human materials. Ignore for a few minutes the grand human narratives and attend to the layers of Martian dust on the windowsills, or to moonlight in the puddles. Walk as if you were out of your depth for a while.*

Gently revolving in a universe of dead and dying stars, dominated by stasis, silence and stillness and the slow and elephantine shifting of cyclopean forces, it is perhaps not surprising that a philosophical and cultural dualism, separating an unworldly and smoky inwardness of self and soul from an outer universe of clunky deadness, might gain some favour over time. Hans Jonas's characterisation that "[L]ife dwells like a stranger in the flesh" (p.13) captures something of an almost Gnostic self that can only be liberated when released from the tomb of its body by death or imagination.

The living dead, however, tell us something different: that this stranger in the flesh that we call "life" *is* the flesh. That there is nothing else *but* the alien and cosmic tomb of the body, and that the silences, vacuums and monstrous structures of the universe are not only out there, they are, also, in here, in us. In fact, more than that, they *are* us.

> *Walk in deep time. Slow your pace and feel historic time race by, overtake you and disappear into the distance. Stop and feel a succession of deserts, oceans and ice fields slide beneath your feet. Feel the core burn your body away. Become gas, whirled backwards and then around in the unpeeling of the Earth; feel the Moon slam into your body. Walk until the light draws in. Walk through the evening and into the night, allowing*

everything to close in around you and on you. Then in the darkness feel the loss of differentiation, the surge of plasma, reach out to the thickening density of the darkness, until you sense your imminent arrival at a place where explanations break down, somewhere unrepresentable.

Then turn on your torch and find your way home; perhaps taking in a café snack or a drink in a bar on the way. Be ordinary, everyday and everything for a while.

I'm not the only one to spot this cosmic-corporeal implication in the Romero mythos. In his screenplay for Savini's 1990 remake of 'Night', as I noted above, Romero has Barbara watch rednecks shoot zombies for entertainment at a congregating that is rather like a County Fair and then has her remark, almost to herself, in realisation: "They're us. We're them". These same words, not approximately but *exactly*, are used by Gary Sinese's astronaut character in Brian De Palma's 'Mission to Mars' (2000), not about rednecks, but watching a holographic account of the Martians seeding the Earth with DNA.

When confronted by the infected in Max Brooks's *World War Z*, an Israeli professor calls them 'golems', qualifying his judgement with "these weren't made from clay" (p.33). The professor was right the first time. Just because these 'golems' are not "docile and obedient" does not mean that they have not come to us via the river bank. Unlike Donna Haraway's cyborg which "is not made of mud and cannot dream of returning to dust" (p.151), the living dead are like the bad dream of Christian white supremacists; the mud people we all are, made from the dust of dead stars. Our flesh is geological.

Walk as if you were red sandstone. Walk as grey limestone. Walk your body as if it were composed of the geology around you; because it is. Be volatile, then metamorphic, sedimentary, and, finally, faulted.

Look for things as partners to walk with. Once you have found a first thing, carry it until you find another; leave the first and pick up the second, carry it until you find a third, and so on. On the beach I carried seaweed, changed it for a handful of red earth from an ornamental garden, headed inland and exchanged the last dried crumbs of earth for a stick that I threw in the air, then a plastic disc that I span through the sky, and finally I bought a tiny oil painting for £1 in a second-hand shop, took it to the seashore, beachcombed jetsam and made a collage of it.

By imagining that inanimate things are in some way separate from, or of lower value than, us, setting our life above their non-life, we are stupidly walking back into that gothic conflict in one body that is the living dead, what Elizabeth Povinelli calls 'the carbon imaginary'. She describes how, by telling ourselves a story about birth, reproductive sex (which is where Bruce LaBruce makes his separation from this Separation) and death, we create an isolated farmhouse for ourselves, young adults upstairs, Family in the cellar, corpse on the landing, and attempt to maintain the 'things as they are' against the things outside that "are coming to get [us]". With species self-interest on the one hand and tales of a wounded goddess seeking revenge on the other, we imagine we sever ourselves from the things that control us, the oil that controls human politics far more than human politics controls oil – things that we might influence more if only we stopped nailing up the windows and turning on a screen to watch more pictures of ourselves in a panic.

The speculative realist Graham Harman argues that "[T]he inherent stupidity of all content" does not preclude knowledge given that even an "absent thing-in-itself can have gravitational effects on the internal content of knowledge" (p.17). The philosopher Dylan Trigg draws on just such gravitational effects made by alien bodies in the flux of popular culture, analysing materials and patterns from Hammer's 'Quatermass and the Pit' (1967) and John Carpenter's 'The Thing' (1982), and triangulating his findings with information from meteor studies and Maurice Merleau-Ponty to support a phenomenological study of human bodies as ancient, alien sites. The pull of bodies like Bub or Number 9, or indeed that of any zombie, would do just as well. Trigg's description of a "depersonalized assemblage of alien matter to some extent already dead before it has come to life... [a] body... constituted by a plane of anonymous existence irreducible to experience and opposed to our concept of what is 'human'" (p.58) *is* the Romero zombie, the zombie that was always in us, a revenant from almost the beginning of a universe that is "both constitutive of humanity and also *against humanity*" (p.12).

> *You might try a walk against the brightening sun.*
>
> *In 'Remains', zombies slip into sleep once the sun has set, allowing the living characters to walk warily among them. In 'Wyrmwood' the living dead 'selfishly' cease to belch flammable and exploitable gases in the dark and, instead, use them to power themselves, shifting their pace from daylight shamble to*

nocturnal sprint. This turns the mythos upside down; with Day preceding and relegating Night to a subtraction of energy.

Walk towards the sun and hopelessly deny it a setting. Prise it from its regularity. Stride to the horizon in pursuit.

Hide in the shadows on a hot summer's day; make your way through rooms and corridors without windows, along tunnels, travel by metro, visit the basement floors of stores, suck ice cubes in bars, cool down at the doorways of giant freezers.

Trace a route of chilliness in the bright, hot city.

Walk through shadows as if they were strand lines, noting what you might beachcomb in the event of social breakdown; consider how you might exchange contact, communication, sociability and stories for things. Wandering about New York in the aftermath of Hurricane Sandy, I came upon a grocery store on a housing project; a notice apologised for its closure explaining that its tills were down. They had food, they had change, but they were not able to communicate with the rest of the money system. As you move from pool of darkness to pool of darkness, consider what currencies, other than money and prostituted sex, you will communicate in, when the current structure is bitten. Stories, labour, knowledge, songs, analyses, directions, recipes... what else?

What Hans Jonas calls an interloper in the body is the 'Life' that human culture has devised so many feints and dodges to keep ahead of, sprinting away like Columbus in the pedagogical opening to 'Zombieland'. This is the splinter in the organism that Emmanuel Levinas describes in terms of insomnia: "one cannot say that there is an 'I' which cannot manage to fall asleep. The impossibility of escaping wakefulness is something 'objective'... I do not stay awake: 'it' stays awake" (p.49, Levinas). Similarly, Mario Perniola appeals to something "implicit and essential" in human affect that "compel[s] us to say: 'one feels', but prevent[s] us from saying 'I feel'" (p.8).

This is the vitalism we share with the zombie, the geological and ancient inanimateness that drives it and us, chopped off from the organising logic of an organism. Which is why speculations about the physiology of individual zombies – not being able to run because their legs would snap, and so on – are always absurd, even in their own terms. Logic only applies to zombies when they are expressed as a mass and in relation to "conditions wherein a global, civilisation-ending event is possible" (p.23, Saunders). Instead, if we apply this ancient and alien vitalism to ourselves, then the possibilities for collectivity and radical change are revived, not on the basis of our exploitation of a productive surplus, but rather on how we achieve a reparative relationship with our ancient and alien Earth. The zombie is a nonsense fiction that, by an absurd reduction and subtraction of life reveals a 'Life' we demean by our Cartesian privileging of mind over body: "a zombie is a zero level of humanity, the inhuman/mechanical core of humanity" (p.100, Gabriel & Žižek).

Remake yourself, using zeroes.

In the recent past, radical change was proposed on the basis of the liberation of humans, the equalisation of relations and the escape from necessity. By interpreting the clues within a trashy apocalypse, the next great movement for change will be characterised by our binding ourselves to the reparation of things, attending to the ancient and alien thing in ourselves, committing ourselves to the gratifying embrace of necessity and the embrace of the necessity of gratification, abandoning humanism and anthropomorphic gods in favour of thick nothingness, passing structural legislation in favour of slowness and intensity rather than acceleration, developing new disciplines of sociability and a citizenship, home and city without boundaries; plus the rearrangement of the senses.

Find your way to the place where the gap between what is

129

supposedly outside you and what is inside is smallest. Create a third entity where the usual distinctions between soft ideas and hard things can drop away; until you can walk on concepts and think in bollards. Walk with a neutral dimension and let 'it' keep you awake to everything around you.

We cannot step far enough away from the body – human, alien or zombie – in order to study it, for we walk enmeshed with its conceptual meat, "as if we did not feel in the first person but only in that indeterminable and porous thing we have become", (p77, Perniola). We must shoot destination in the head (the only way to kill it) and invent each next place, on the hoof, from the clay of the fields, the mud of the river and the dust of the road.

When you walk like a zombie, you are treading a path between the contradictions the cosmos has dealt you.

Seek out a landscape that can perform them for you.

Somewhere that can make real for you the vast silences and stases of the universe, the elephantine shifts of cyclopean forces. Perhaps walking a new motorway before it is opened to traffic. Or the bed of a drained lake. The ruin of a redundant quarry. The loft of a cathedral. The ritual routes laid out in now fallen stones on moors. An abandoned production line. An empty theatre. A sand bank. .

When you are there, try to practice that idea of the Kyoto philosophers about experiencing without analysing, unknowing sensitivity. Imagine new senses (renew very old ones).

Then walk back to busy, public spaces, ones like those I walked through coming out of 'Dawn of the Dead' in Coventry in 1980. Walk without display. Walk silent, cold, distant, and echoing.

Attend a zombie walk or zombie parade, one where people dress up and make up; but dress down and make down. Go with the crowd. Don't try to be different or creative. Coolly copy. Follow the route the crowd takes. Walk in cosmic indifference within the parade; not unfriendly but conformist, seeking the cosmic core of the mythos everyone is celebrating, manifesting the philosophical zombie; rock I, oil I; walking the fossil universe.

18/ the step after

In 'Mørke Sjeler', Johanna is being fed by her father, Morten. As he feeds her she responds by chewing each mouthful. But once Morten gets up to answer a phone call, lost without a stimulus from outside herself, she stops eating, eventually slumping into her plate of food. Her behaviour is similar to that of patients famously described by Oliver Sacks in his book *Awakenings* (1973), descriptions interrogated by dance theorist Erin Manning as a means to understanding the dynamics of walking. In her *Relationscapes* (2012), Manning relates how Sacks's patients had become immobilised by a tendency to a "degree-zero of movement" (p.50), a bodily inertia that was not necessarily motionless, but was an inability to shift from one gait or degree to another; they could not change their state. The auto-activation that most people can take for granted, these sufferers could not: for them "[A]ctivation must come from outside" (p.51).

For Johanna in 'Mørke Sjeler', the 'outside' she relied on to act is another person, but for Sacks's patients it could be a particular kind of space. Erin Manning describes how one of the patients, Hester Y., if brought to a set of stairs might suddenly and spontaneously begin to climb them, "but place her in an open space and she will stay stock still... where experiential space-time is 'smooth', Hester cannot move" (p.51). Thinking is not enough to get the patients moving; they cannot ponder their way from absolute to distinct movement. Thought leads them not into a rich and intense nothingness, but into an empty simulacrum: "whatever I think leads deeper and deeper into itself... Everything I do is a map of itself... every part leads into itself... I've got a thought in my mind, and then I see something in it, like a dot on the skyline. It comes nearer and nearer, and then I see what it is – it's just the same thought I was thinking before" (Rose R. quoted by Manning).

The problem for these sufferers is that there is no 'elsewhere' they can imagine that would make their bodies want to move to it. When something like a thought of 'over there' does appear, the closer it is inspected the more it folds back upon itself as a copy of a previous thought. This implosion does not dull the senses, but "it becomes impossible to sense-with. There is no toward to which to relate" (p.53).

Space in the post-1968 living dead movie is similarly smooth; the lurch of the monster and its ability to suddenly arrive up close to a victim depends on flat, easily traversed ground. The zombie is an explosion of sensing-with, launching off with a massive drive 'toward', followed by the immediate predation upon its body of absolute movement. Without a new prey to trip this inertia, the zombie mills about, becalmed, until the stimulus of a new prey begins a distinct motion, until that prey is caught or lost and then absolute movement and inertia again dominate.

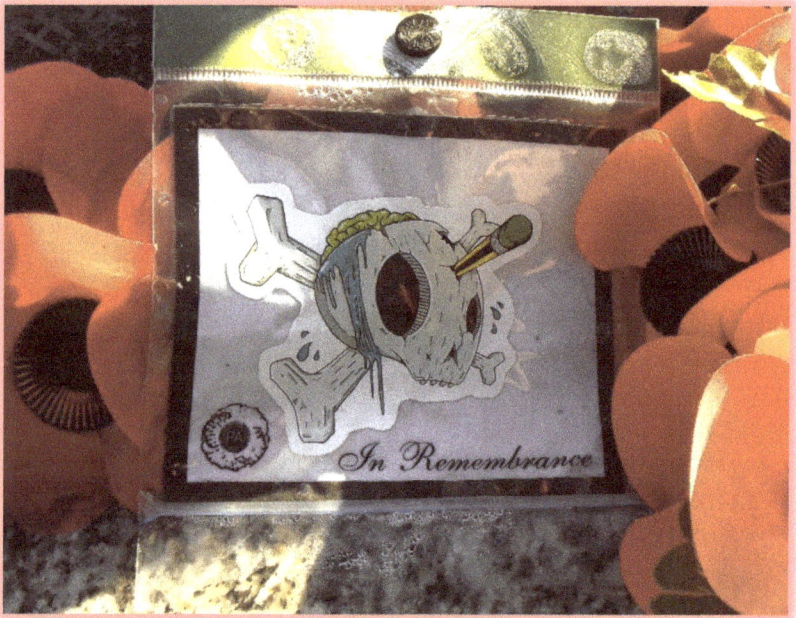

Similarly, when Ana's car, after dodging so many obstacles in the striated space of suburbia under apocalypse, hammers into a tree, the 'Dawn' remake enters its own smooth inner space, represented on the one hand by a mall still under the control of humans, and, on the other, by a sweeping of all the apparent obstacles of indifference, violence, consumption and acceleration under the magic carpet of Islam. The movie never recovers, or at least not until the post-credits sequence when the living dead emerge out of the smooth nowhere of the survivors' island paradise: not the first tourists to discover that their resort is really just an infected suburbia by the sea.

You can use that image of Ana's flight suddenly brought to a halt by the tree, and freeze it there, get out of the vehicle and walk away. You might trip up the zombie fiction's endless making a virtue of its failure to engage with reality; an example of this process, from 'The Walking Dead', is described here by Jennifer Rutherford: "We are suddenly catapulted from the unfolding story... into the killing fields of Rwanda, Bosnia, Cambodia. We know these dead bodies... disinterred from the mass graves of modernity. But interrupting the pleasurable weekly instalment of a zombie TV series makes them momentarily new, REAL, unassimilated. And then attention shifts." (p.14)

> *Slam your viewing into a tree. Before your attention shifts, get out of your seat. Walk away.*

The freedoms, varieties and hyper-accelerated communications of digital globalisation mask a tendency towards an absolute movement of infolding sensing-self and smooth space. A striking example of this is the character still listening to his downloaded music as he is eaten alive in 'Colin', unable to escape absolute movement despite his pain.

> *To take the next step, walk-with the world. As you follow that first step with another, fold your thoughts out to the world around you. Choose spaces of roughness, ones with obstacles, otherness and every kind of scratch and marking to get purchase upon and explore. Take the unevenness and alienness of the terrain under your feet up into the top of your head, let it mark through the thickness of your body, and then fold it out once more to the immediate terrain and take a further step. If you feel the inertia of smooth thinking starting to fold you in and close you down, choose a new obstacle to navigate. For each step that you are taking, you are making a relation to something; bring that relation to something to the front of your thoughts and watch it change at each step. Keep varying and changing that 'something'. Imagine a new relation and make the connection. Take the next step. Then, allow the thing-in-itself within you, that ancient thing, to begin to feel out and reach out, to the thing-in-the-world; walk with past reaching out to future through the thickness of your flesh.*

One of Sachs's patients, Frances D., found that she had a tendency to freeze in the long corridor of her hospital. For such emergencies she carried with her a few balls of screwed up paper; whenever she felt inertia falling upon her she would throw one of the balls ahead and this would restart her next step. Carry paper balls or some equivalent, mental or material, to use whenever you feel inertia or infolding, or sense the encroaching smoothness of an ideological space. Put down your obstacles, create your own grip and resistance.

Make large and small obstacles to carry, put down and climb over. Carry symbolic materials that remind you to walk-with the things-in-the-world. Take a whole phantasmagoria for a walk. Be a corporeal symbolist, not 'floating free' your symbols this time, but walking-with them to others. Take the next step.

Erin Manning asserts that "walking is all about taking the next step" (p.49) and that crucial to each next step is "to step with the feeling of walking", to be *in* the act, mentally-physically, sensing the nature of the obstacles, frictions, fictions, *frissons* and vistas around you and in you without, or before, having to directly touch or taste them. Each next step requires that "we move-with the feeling of the ground as it expands towards the pelvis, giving into the weight of gravity's pull... We move-with the edge of a room approaching or the horizon line receding. To take the next step is to move-with the world" (p.49).

Walk away.

In Tom Savini's 1990 remake of 'Night of the Living Dead', Barbara quickly identifies just how "messed up" the dead really are: "they're so slow... we could walk right past them, we wouldn't even need to run... I'm fighting, not panicking". She is right. It is possible to get past them with little effort and thereby avoid getting boxed in at the farmhouse; by walking in a careful relation to these living dead it is possible to evade them and to find other humans. Rather than being sucked into confrontations with tiny numbers of the dead in enclosed spaces, Barbara's suggested "fighting" is performance-like in its to-the-sideness. No one listens to Barbara. As a result, her companions die in or around the farmhouse. But Barbara does escape and walks past the pedestrian dead, switching expertly between the smoothness of retreat and moments of intense and striated confrontation.

She walks away. Her escape is not an emotionally simple one, but it is successful and, at the end of it, she finds a new, alien and unexpected community with whom to begin again.

> *The farmhouse used as location for the first 'Night' was demolished shortly after filming. Today, on the site of what the film crew called 'The Monster House' are acres and acres of smooth turf, produced for the laying of lawns, what in the US is called a 'sod farm'.*

> *Walk in anonymous, manicured, levelled, official, gated and recently industrialised spaces. Imagine the zombie spaces that were once there, before you gave up thinking apocalyptically. The farmhouse traps, the animal pens, the welcoming malls, the infested housing projects. Walk like an archaeologist through these historic relics of the imagination. Rethink history as an anticipation, not an interment. Examine these ideological artefacts as a past you can leave behind; respect, but leave behind: "rethinking an idea of revolution capable of interrupting the disastrous course of things is to purge it of every apocalyptic element it has contained up to now" (p.38, The Invisible Committee). It is time for the zombie uprising to eat itself. And be still.*

In her early scenes in the 1990 'Night', Barbara does little to suggest the hope and agency she will find by the end of the movie. Perhaps to emphasise her transformation – what Romero described as his "apology to women" (quoted, p.259, Blumberg & Hershburger) for the stereotypical victimhood and passivity of the original Barbra – she is shown still deeply mired in oppressive stereotypes. In the cemetery, rather than the Karloff-like teasing of the original movie, Johnny instead taunts: "they're horny, Barbara, they've been dead a long time!" When the zombies attack they noticeably follow a familiar model, common to zombie movies as disparate as 'The Living Dead at the Manchester Morgue' (1974) and 'Tokyo Zombie' (2005): it is "an attempted rape... [the] attack on her is an attack on not just a human [that the zombie] wishes to bite and eat, but an attack on a female" (p.50, Wetmore).

> *Walk away. Walk past the zombie movies. Walk past the stereotypical figures. They are phantasms and they are slow.*

You can evade them if you walk carefully in relation to them. You can rob them of their phantasmic survival by refusing them your spectatorship. There is a quite different 'Land Of' beyond the malignant gaze of spectators.

In the opening scene of Romero's 'Land' we see a group of zombies tooting and harrumphing on musical instruments in a bandstand; across the way Big Daddy, a deceased petrol attendant emerges with a severed gas nozzle in hand. He and his female counterpart, Number 9, will *lead* a nomad gang of these dead on a mission of predation into the gated city and against its wealthy and powerful. But then, unexpectedly, they seem to reject predation against humans in general (or at least against the 99%) and, instead, set off on a far less certain collective wander; just to "find a place" as a human character observes.

Walk away.

One explanation for the shuffle of the zombie walk is that it is a remnant of the slaves' saving of energy; a subtly resistant act (a conservation passing itself off as exhaustion) against the modernist industrialisation of plantation labour. A *détournement* of the idea of efficiency on the slaves' own terms. These are hopelessly compromised materials, recuperable only in despair.

Walk away.

In Lori Allen Ohm's stage adaptation of 'Night', premiered in 2000, first the living dead, and then Chief McClellan's posse, enter through the audience and take to the stage: "everything bad comes from us – the audience" (p.110, Wetmore). Not only does Ben die in Ohm's version, but by the end so have all the vigilantes. As the final human expires, for the first time the audience is seen by the living dead. The zombies pause, turn and gaze out into the auditorium. The malevolent gaze is finally returned, from the infected terrain of the theatre – "We have seen *Night* before, but for the first time *Night* is seeing us" (p.110) – in this moment the mythos is revived to indict and insist to life those who can be more than spectators.

Walk away.

19/ other resources

I probably should recommend some handbooks on how to survive the zombie apocalypse, but they, perhaps understandably, mostly restrict themselves to tactics for survival and more survival and then a bit more survival; repeating the accumulative behaviour that has delivered us up to the risk of extinction in the first place. More zombie product unable to escape its bunker.

Far better to look for resources in the absurd margins of the mythos. For example, dancing: in 'Carnival of Souls' (1962), 'Thriller' (1983), 'The Happiness of the Katakuris" (2001) ("always keep moving, even if no one is waiting for you") and the boogying buttered zombies of Laura Shigihara's bubblegum pop video 'Zombies On Your Lawn' for the 'Plants vs Zombies' game (tag line: 'get ready to soil your plants').

There are also numerous walks from the movies to borrow: Shaun's de-sensitised routine trip to the shops, and his equally direct group trip across the back gardens, Barbra's rush across the countryside from the cemetery swivelling as she goes to take in more and more of the landscape, the nod to 'Dawn' in the low budget 'Colin' when a survivor uses a supermarket trolley to make his way, Glenn Rhee's slipping in and out of infested Atlanta, Vincent Price following a dog ('Life') and finding space (a new species), Jim's wary walk through an 'empty' central London, the group's escape from a dull student soap opera in their domestic bunker and then their sublime journeying out of the city in 'Darkest Day' (2015), and, if only for sheer bathos, the dead prisoners who rise from a mass grave in the execrable 'Shadow: Dead Riot' (2006) only to shamble back behind bars.

20/ in conclusion

"The human race tends to remember the abuses to which it has been subjected rather than the endearments. What's left of kisses? Wounds, however, leave scars." (Bertolt Brecht, 'The Trial of Lucullus', 1940)

"Why don't you write about something nice?" (My mum, many times.)

Part of the trick of 'survival plus' is to ignore the apocalypse and its timetable. If we spend our time trying to predict the moment when catastrophe will slide over the edge of the basin of attraction we will always be both too late and too early for playful walking. Better to start surviving the apocalypse that is happening right now, making the fine mesh connections that might hold enough things together for the time being, not for when the foundations go. This might not have the same dark romance as necessity and horror, but prefigurative actions have plenty of light pleasures when driven by dispersed hedonism. The grounds of such 'unnecessary' survivalism will be our bodies; eating selfishly and planting sociably, moving more slowly in order to arrive at all, shortening physical travel but imagining further, practising empathy and organising an ethics of strangers (trading in whom, and in whose affections, is unacceptable).

Here the living dead mythos is helpful. Less for its successful metaphors, more for what it does not deal well with: the obscured colonial remnant's return, the inconsistencies of the collective, the unresolved conflations of master/subject and slave/object in its posthumanism, the absorption of erotic, morbid and enslaved stiffness in its walk, and its collapsing in on its own spectacle (in 'Mimesis' [2011] where 'Night of the Living Dead' is replayed in role play murders or the opening of 'Wyrmwood' where a model made up as a ghoul for a photo shoot becomes a ghoul). In its troubles we confront our own. Facing these inadequacies and inarticulacies we, necessarily, leave the material world mostly unchanged; what does change, however, in the terms of Merleau-Ponty's phenomenology, is 'flesh': the dead thing that is in us calling out to the other dead things in the world.

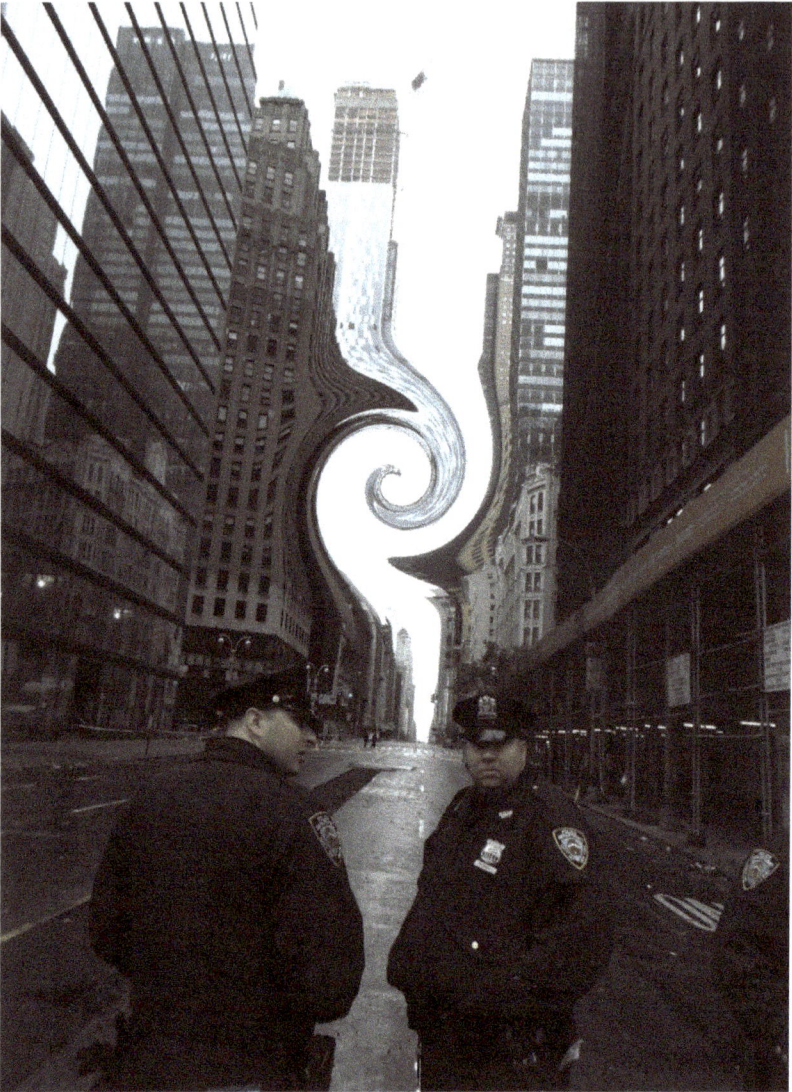

When the 'flesh' changes, the mouth changes; from consuming to consummate. Turn your face, with Number 9's and Big Daddy's, away from the fireworks and towards unity with the road.

Walk without words.

Walk with that 'thingness' that Julia Kristeva describes as the residue of our identification with the world, expressed every day in our bodies' unconscious emissions, tics and twitches, the material part of the body independent of language, the automatism within our subjectivity (p.134).

Walk embarrassed.

In 'Pontypool' (2008), in a talk radio station, a language-born virus strikes, first turning its carriers into concrete poets and then into monsters dominated by their thingness. The genius of the film is that when this automatism turns on the bodies of its characters, those bodies are able to deploy a new speech to bring themselves back from absolute movement, absolute language. Sometimes by inversion, sometimes by to-the-sideness, sometimes by a floating free:

> "So here we go, folks: 'Kill' is 'Kiss', 'Kill' is definitely 'Kiss'... Now, 'Sample' is 'Staple'..."
>
> "Sweetheart..."
>
> "It's too specific, Grant..."
>
> "Sidney Briar! Are you still alive? Listen to me, folks – everything is something else."
>
> "Okay?"
>
> "Sidney Briar! Are you still alive? If you are saying 'Happy', it means 'Sad'... 'Happy' means... no that's the opposite, it can't be that. 'Happy' is 'Handy'... 'Happy' is 'Handy'. Move things around, people. Just move it around, just... You have to stop understanding..."

> *Walk without attention to signs. Walk misinterpreting signs. Read concretely rather than linguistically. Follow directions according to the shapes of the letters rather than the place they name. Engage passers-by in conversations in which you introduce 'thingness', concrete poetry and inversions; without making fun of your new acquaintances, privilege the turn over the phrase, the juxtaposition over the position.*

Walk with these ideas and you walk with a fossil inside your face, you walk with fleets of alien invasions rippling up and down your veins and in and out of your heart, you walk terrorformed, and you walk in refusal of a morbid world, ready for the transformation to a new one where "kill means kiss".

Then go and do something else.

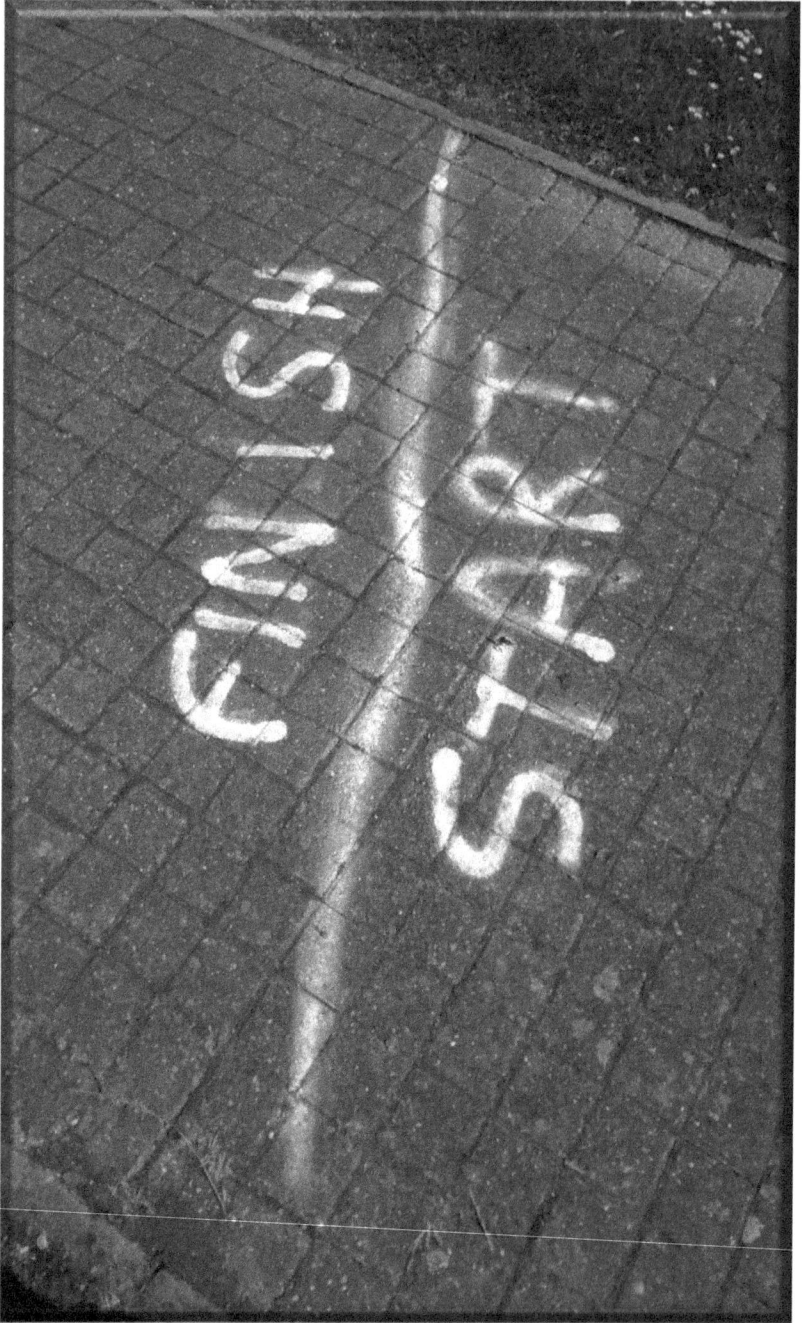

Bibliography

Anonymous (1980) *20th Century City & Urban Survival*, BPCC
Wheatons

Asma, Stephen T. (2009) *On Monsters: an unnatural history of our worst fears*, Oxford University Press

Bacon, Simon (2013) 'How the Earth went bad: from Wells' 'War of the Worlds' to the zombie apocalypse in the 21st century' in *Monstrous Geographies: places and spaces of the monstrous*. (eds.) Mostin, Sarah & Evelyn Tsitas, Inter-Disciplinary Press

Barber, Stephen (2014) *Performance Projections: film and the body in action*, Reaktion Books

Baser, Shumon, Douglas Coupland and Hans Ulich Obrist (2015) *The Age of Earthquakes: a guide to extreme present*, Penguin Books

Baudelaire, Charles (1947) *Paris Spleen*, New Directions

Billinghurst, Carla (2015) 'The Usual Precautions I – The Australian Zombie Apocalypse', in *Halibut, Herring & You*, self-published

Blumberg, Arnold T. & Andrew Hershburger (2006) *Zombiemania*. Tolworth: Telos

Brooks, Max (2006) *World War Z: an oral history of the zombie war*, Duckworth

Brooks, Max & Ibraim Roberson (2009) *The Zombie Survival Guide: Recorded Attacks*, Duckworth Overlook

Burgess, Tony (1995) *Pontypool Changes Everything*, ECW Press

Careri, Francesco (2002) *Walkscapes*. Barcelona: Editorial Gustavo Gili

Carter, Robert E. (2013) *The Kyoto School: an introduction*, State University of New York Press

Clark, Simon (2006) 'The undead martyr' in *The Undead and Philosophy: chicken soup for the soulless.* (eds.) Greene, Richard & K. Silem Mohammad, Open Court

Coates, Ta-Nehisi (2015) *Between the World and Me* Text Publishing

Cohen, Josh (2013) *The Private Life: why we remain in the dark,* Granta

de Certeau, Michel (1998) *The Practice of Everyday Life* (trans. Steven Rendall) University of California Press

Deleuze, Gilles (1997) *Negotiations 1972-1990* (trans. Martin Joughin) Columbia University Press

Deleuze, Gilles & Felix Guattari (2004) *A Thousand Plateaus* (trans. Brian Massumi) Continuum

DeSilvey, Caitlin, Simon Naylor & Colin Sackett (eds.) (2011) *Anticipatory History,* Uniform Books

Deslandes, Ann & Kristian Adamson (2013) 'Zombie Solidarity' in *Zombies in the Academy: living death in higher education* (eds.) Whelan, Andrew, Ruth Walker & Christopher Moore, Intellect

Dixon, Wheeler Winston (2003) *Visions of the Apocalypse,* Wallflower Press

Do Vale, Simone (2010) 'Trash Mob: zombie walks and the positivity of minsters in Western culture' in *The Domination of Fear* (ed.) Canini, Mikko, Rodopi

Fincham, Ben, Mark McGuinness & Lesley Murray (2010) *Mobile Methodologies,* Palgrave Macmillan

Foucault, Michel (1995) *Discipline and Punish* (trans. Alan Sheridan) Vintage

Gabriel, Markus & Slavoj Žižek (2009) *Mythology, Madness and Laughter: subjectivity in German Idealism,* Continuum

Goodall, Mark (2012) 'The Politics and Poetics of the Italian Zombie Film' in *European Nightmares: horror cinema in Europe since 1945.* (eds.) Allmer, Patricia, Emily Brick & David Huxley, Wallflower Press

Gray, Todd (ed.) (2001) *Victorian Ghost Stories,* The Mint Press

Haden, David (2011) *Walking With Cthulhu: H. P. Lovecraft as a psychogeographer*, self-published

Halberstam, Judith (2006) *Skin Shows: gothic horror and the technology of monsters*, Duke University Press

Haraway, Donna (1991) *Simians, Cyborgs and Women*, Routledge

Harman, Graham (2012) *Weird Realism: Lovecraft and Philosophy*, Zero Books

Hawkins, Harriet & Elizabeth Straughan (2015) *Geographical Aesthetics: imagining space, staging encounters*, Ashgate

Hervey, Ben (2008) *Night of the Living Dead*, BFI/Palgrave Macmillan

Horkeimer, Max & Theodor W. Adorno (2002) *Dialectic of Enlightenment: philosophical fragments* (trans. Edmund Jephcott) Stanford University Press

Hunter, Victoria (2015) 'Spatial translation, embodiment and the site-specific event' in *Moving Sites: investigating site-specific dance performance* (ed.) Hunter, Victoria, Routledge

Irven, Donovan, 'Anarchism of the Living Dead', accessed 16.4.15, www.academia.edu/2779260/Anarchism_of_the-Living-Dead

Jonas, Hans (2001) *The Phenomenon of Life*, Northwestern University Press

Jones, Steve (2010) *Zombie Apocalypse*, Constable & Robinson

Killjoy, Margaret (2012) *A Steampunk's Guide to The Apocalypse*, Combustion Books

Kristeva, Julia (1989) *Black Sun: depression and melancholia*, Columbia University Press

Land, Nick (2012) *Fanged Noumena: collected writings 1987-2007*, Urbanomic/Sequence

Lauro, Sarah Juliet & Karen Embry (2008) 'A zombie manifesto: the non-human condition in the era of advanced capitalism', *boundary* 2, 35:1, Duke University Press

Lauro, Sarah Juliet (2013) "Sois mort et tais toi". In *Zombies In The Academy: living death in higher education* (eds.) Whelan, Andrew, Ruth Walker & Christopher Moore, Intellect

Levinas, Emmanuel (1985) *Ethics and Infinity* (trans. Richard Cohen) Duquesne University Press

Luckhurst Roger (2015) *Zombies: a cultural history*, Reaktion Books

Manning, Erin (2012) *Relationscapes*, The MIT Press

Marcelo, Leon (2006) *Creepy Crawls: a horror fiend's travel guide*, Santa Monica Press

May, Jeff (2010) 'Zombie geographies and the undead city', *Social & Cultural Geography*, 11:3

Merrifield, Andy (2011) *Magical Marxism: subversive politics and the imagination*, Pluto Press

McHugh, Maureen F (2011) *After the Apocalypse*, Small Beer Press

Miller, Lee (2014) 'Playing (un)dead', *Studies in Theatre and Performance*, 34: 3, Routledge

Morgan, Jack (2002) *The Biology of Horror: gothic literature and film*, Southern Illinois University Press

Negarestani, Rexa (2008) *Cyclonopedia: complicity with anonymous materials*, Re:press

Newman, Kim (1988) *Nightmare Movies: horror on screen since the 1960s*, Bloomsbury

Nishitani, Keiji (1983) *Religion and Nothingness* (trans. Jan Van Bragt) University of California Press

Page, Sean T. & Ian Moore (2013) *Zombie Survival Manual*, Haynes Publishing

Perniola, Mario (2004) *Sex Appeal of the Inorganic*, (trans. Massimo Verdicchio) Continuum

Pulliam, June (2007) 'The zombie' in *Icons of Horror and the Supernatural*. (ed.) S. T. Joshi, Greenwood

Romero, George A. & Tony Williams (ed.) (2011) *George A. Romero: Interviews*, University Press of Mississippi

Russell, Jamie (2005) *Book of the Dead: the complete history of zombie cinema*, FAB Press

Rutherford, Jennifer (2013) *Zombies*, Routledge

Saunders, Robert A. (2013) 'Zombies in the Colonies: Imperialism and Contestation of Ethno-Political Space in Max Brooks' *The Zombie Survival Guide*' in *Monstrous Geographies: places and spaces of the monstrous* (eds.) Montin, Sarah & Evelyn Tsitas, Inter-Disciplinary Press

Shoard, Marion (2002) 'Edgelands' in *Remaking The Landscape: the changing face of Britain* (ed.) Jennifer Jenkins, Profile Books

Smith, Phil (2010) *Mythogeography*, Triarchy Press

_____(2012) 'History, Terrain and Tread: the walk of demons, zombie flesh eaters and the blind dead' in *European Nightmares: horror cinema in Europe since 1945*. (Eds.) Allmer, Patricia, Emily Brick & David Huxley, Wallflower Press

_____'Performative walking in zombie towns', in *Studies in Theatre and Performance*, 34: 3, Routledge

_____(2015) *Walking's New Movement*, Triarchy Press

_____(submitted) 'A taxonomy of 'zombie space' for walking in monstrous cities' in *Horror Studies*, Intellect

_____(in press) 'Using Zombies to Teach Theatre Students' in *Teaching Monsters*, (eds.) Heather Hayton & Adam Golub, McFarland: due 2016

Solnit, Rebecca (2000) *Wanderlust: a history of walking*, Viking

Sontag, Susan (2009) *Against Interpretation*, Penguin Classics

Thacker, Eugene (2015) *Tentacles Longer Than Night*, Zero Books

The Invisible Committee (2015) *To Our Friends*, semiotext(e)

Trigg, Dylan (2014) *The Thing: a phenomenology of horror*, Zero Books

Virilio, Paul (1997) 'The overexposed city' in *Rethinking Architecture: a reader in cultural history* (ed.) Leech, N., Routledge

Wark, McKenzie (2013) *50 Years of Recuperation of the Situationist International*, Buell Center/FORuM Project & Princeton Architectural Press

Wetmore, Kevin J. (2011) *Back from the Dead: remakes of the Romero zombie films as markers of their times*, McFarland

Williams, Evan Calder (2011) *Combined and Uneven Apocalypse*, Zero Books

Bibliography

Žižek, Slavoj (1992) *Enjoy Your Symptom!: Jacques Lacan in Hollywood and out*, Routledge

_____(2007) 'The family myth in Hollywood', *Cinephile* Vol.3, Number 1, Spring/Summer 2007

_____(2008) *In Defence of Lost Causes,* Verso

About the Author

Dr Phil Smith is a prolific writer, performer, urban mis-guide, dramaturg [for TNT Munich], counter-tourist, drifter, artist-researcher and academic. He has written or co-written over one hundred professionally produced works for a wide range of British and international theatres and touring companies, and has created and performed in numerous site-specific theatre projects, often with Exeter-based Wrights & Sites, of which he is a core member [**www.mis-guide.com**]. He has collaborated recently with choreographers Melanie Kloetzel, Siriol Joyner and Jane Mason on performances and explorations.

He is Associate Professor (Reader) in the School of Humanities and Performing Arts at Plymouth University.

Phil has published papers in *Studies In Theatre and Performance, Performance Research, Cultural Geographies*, and *New Theatre Quarterly* and co-authored a range of Mis-Guides with the other members of Wrights & Sites. He has written or co-written a number of other books including: *On Walking… and Stalking Sebald; Enchanted Things; Mythogeography: A Guide to Walking Sideways; Counter-Tourism: The Handbook; A Sardine Street Book of Tricks; Walking's New Movement; Walking, Writing & Performance* and the novel *Alice's Dérives in Devonshire*.

www.triarchypress.net/smithereens

About the Publisher

Triarchy Press is an independent publisher of alternative thinking (altThink) about government, finance, organisations, society, movement, performance, walking, somatics, the future, the creative life and, now, zombies.

www.triarchypress.net

www.ingramcontent.com/pod-product-compliance
Lightning Source LLC
Chambersburg PA
CBHW040137270326
41927CB00020B/3432